the POLITICAL IMAGE Merchants:

Strategies in the NEW POLITICS

PUBLISHED BY **ACROPOLIS BOOKS LTD.**/WASHINGTON, D.C. 20009

the
POLITICAL
IMAGE
Merchants:
Strategies in the NEW POLITICS

Edited by

RAY HIEBERT, ROBERT JONES, ERNEST LOTITO, and JOHN LORENZ

WITH FOREWORDS BY
LAWRENCE O'BRIEN
ROBERT J. DOLE
ROGERS C. B. MORTON

CONTEMPORARY ISSUES IN JOURNALISM
Volume I: Politics and the Press
Volume II: Why Aren't We Getting Through?
Volume III: The Political Image Merchants

EDITORIAL BOARD

Ray Eldon Hiebert, Chairman

© *Copyright 1971, Department of Journalism, University of Maryland*

ACROPOLIS BOOKS
*Colortone Building, 2400 17th St., N.W.
Washington, D.C. 20009*

Printed in the United States of America by
COLORTONE PRESS, Creative Graphics Inc.
Washington, D.C. 20009

*Type set in Bodoni and Caledonia
by Colortone Typographic Division, Inc.*

Design by Design and Art Studio 2400, Inc.

Library of Congress Catalog Number 76-148048

Standard Book No. 87491-314-4 (cloth)
87491-315-2

Contents

Editors' Preface

The "new politics" was the big news of the 1970 political campaign. Countless news stories and political interpreters described the political scene in 1970 as one being reshaped by a combination of mass media, sophisticated public opinion analysis, and computers. *Newsweek* magazine stated: "It is fair to say that the medium *is* much of the message in this fall's elections—the selling of the candidates in 1970 is in many respects a more compelling story than their politics."

The success and failure of the new techniques used in 1970 are having enormous implications for the presidential campaign of 1972. These tactics are now not only being perfected; they are also the subject of detailed study, heated debate, and proposed legislation.

In this climate, a month after the 1970 general elections, some one hundred persons gathered at the University of Maryland for a weekend *Conference on Communication Strategies in the New Politics.* This book is the result of that conference.

The conference was an effort to provide a reasonably objective and nonpartisan forum for discussion of the new political approaches and techniques that had gained both widespread use and considerable notoriety in the decade of the 1960's.

True practitioners of the new politics were relatively few in number. And, although they enjoyed a considerable reputation, they remained somewhat mysterious figures whose services were expensive and therefore often unavailable to all but a few political candidates. They also came under frequent attack from those who didn't believe there were "new" ways to elect candidates.

Earlier in the year, Dr. Ray Eldon Hiebert, chairman of the Journalism Department at the University of Maryland,

and Ernest A. Lotito, then a member of the staff of Senator Joseph Tydings, decided that a conference exploring this topic would be both timely and significant. Robert F. Jones and John d'Arc Lorenz, each with specialties in aspects of the new politics, were recruited to help plan the conference. They were joined later by W. Thomas Engram and James P. Baker of the University's Conferences and Institutes Division, Center of Adult Education. The conference was held on December 4, 5, and 6, 1970, under the sponsorship of the Journalism Department.

A balanced group of panelists and speakers—all of them well qualified to discuss the subject—served as the nucleus of the conference. Participants came from 25 states, Hawaii included, and the District of Columbia as well as Canada.

Eight University of Maryland professors played vital roles in the conference, serving as moderators and rapporteurs. They were Dr. Don C. Piper, professor and chairman of the Department of Government and Politics, and Drs. L. John Martin, Lee M. Brown, Charles C. Flippen II, James E. Grunig, Edmund M. Midura, Michael J. Petrick, and Richard W. Lee, all professors of journalism.

Special gratitude is owed to Janis Kinsman, Margaret Markfield, Cheryl Wagner, Roselyn Hiebert, and Arthur Green, for their help in typing transcripts and manuscripts.

This book does not answer all the questions about the new politics. But it does present the current thinking of many of the leading practitioners of the art and science and of some of its most perceptive analysts. Hopefully it will lead to further inquiry and more discussion. Out of this review should come a better understanding of the process, so that it can be accurately reported to the people, adequately regulated for the public interest, and properly perfected to increase the effectiveness of American politics.

Washington, D.C.   Ray Eldon Hiebert
January 1971   Robert F. Jones
                                    John d'Arc Lorenz
                                    Ernest A. Lotito

The Upheaval in American Politics

by Lawrence F. O'Brien,
Chairman
Democratic National Committee

For a political process that some critics deride as immovable and unchanging, the American democratic system is showing surprising life these days. After more than a decade of active political involvement in Washington, and an even longer apprenticeship in Massachusetts, I cannot recall a comparable period when so many of the traditional assumptions and practices of American politics were in question. To me this is heartening evidence of the basic health and vitality of the American political system.

Consider, for example, the revolutionary impact of modern communications and computer technology on the practice of politics. Never before has it been possible to reach the voters so directly and with such frequency, whether through television and radio or such devices as the computer letter. Never before have we known so much *about* the voters—their opinions, motivations, hopes, and fears—as well as their addresses and telephone numbers accurately listed by computer. If one considers no more than the impact of these technologies, we find certain profound changes in the nature of democratic decision-making, where the contemporary voter is assured of far more information about candidates and issues than was previously possible. More than this, the new technologies have made it more feasible for candidates to operate successfully outside the party structure.

But the present upheaval in American politics goes far beyond modernizing the tools of campaigning, even though these developments capture the headlines most often. For the first time since the Supreme Court handed down its historic decision in *Baker* v. *Carr,* the states, using the 1970 census data, will be redistricting all House of Representative and state legislative districts on the basis of "one man-one vote." The effect of the Court's ruling on the eventual outcome of these redistricting decisions cannot, at this writing, be fully comprehended. Only one thing is certain: the new American political map will be noticeably changed from the one that was drawn a decade ago. And the effects of this new political map will be felt in Washington and our state capitals for the balance of the 20th century.

The 1970 census will also tell us a great deal about changing demographic patterns across the United States. Where are people moving? And *which* people are moving? Who, in fact, is now living in the suburbs? And in rural America? What demographic patterns exist in our central cities? The answers to these questions will tell us much about the next decade of American politics—information that was largely speculative before the completion of the 1970 census.

In the Democratic party, at least, we are in the midst of a historic period of reform and rebuilding of the party structure in the states and on the national level. Our 1972 presidential candidate will be chosen by delegates selected by a process that is fundamentally different from the one used in prior presidential years. The Commision on Party Structure and Delegate Selection of the Democratic National Committee has provided specific guidelines to ensure that all Democratic voters have a full, meaningful, and timely opportunity to participate in the selection of delegates to the National Convention. The process of implementing these guidelines in the states has, in turn, produced a reformed and more responsive party structure. This program of party reform has not been accomplished easily, nor has it been without controversy and disagreement. But I am confident that in the 1972 campaign, when the process has been completed, we will discover a Democratic party that has been significantly strengthened because all interested persons will be able to play a more meaningful role in the nomination of our next presidential candidate.

Simultaneously with this reform of the delegate-selection process, the Rules Commission of the Democratic National Committee has been updating the structure and procedures of the National Convention itself. Convention watchers in 1972 will, I believe, be pleasantly surprised; many of the anachronisms of past conventions will have been eliminated as part of the Rules Commission's effort to ensure a nominating procedure that is equitable, open, and instructive to both delegate and citizen.

Much of the promise that these changes hold out to the American voter depends in large measure upon our ability to devise a far more just and rational system of campaign financing. I have long believed that national elections should be federally financed through a check-off system in which taxpayers would designate whether one dollar of their income tax should go into a federal campaign financing pool. Legislation to establish this system would finally eliminate the private political contribution and its accompanying abuses. President Nixon chose to veto the act limiting the amount of money that could be spent on television and radio in primary and general elections—legislation that would have been a constructive first step in the reform of campaign spending. Let us hope that the President and the Congress are now willing to make meaningful reform of the campaign financing system one of their priority objectives in the 92nd Congress.

Finally, we must continue to strive for greater equity of access to television by the opposition party, to offset in some measure the advantage now enjoyed by the President—whether Republican or Democrat—in promoting the policies of his administration. We must work toward a system where the "loyal opposition" is given at least several opportunities each year to take its case directly to the American people.

The cumulative effect of the many changes now under way in the American political system—as well as those we must still strive to achieve—has only begun to be appreciated, even by those practitioners involved most directly in the process. For this reason we can be grateful to the editors of and contributors to this book. Their wisdom and insight, as set forth in the following pages, will help all of us find our way through this exciting period of American politics.

Making the Parties Effective Engines of Change

by Robert J. Dole, *Chairman*
and Rogers C. B. Morton, *Former Chairman*
Republican National Committee

Instant communications, technological advancements and an increasingly literate population have resulted in the American people being deluged with information of all kinds, including political.

Today the problem is not where to find information or whether there is enough information available, either about a candidate or about an issue.

The problem is that there is too much information, and there is not enough time for the average voter to digest it, or even, for that matter, to learn that it exists. The media themselves have neither the time nor the room to disseminate all that is pertinent.

For that reason, the voter must rely on every technique available to bring to him the information he must have in order to exercise the political judgments necessary to voting intelligently.

The political parties have the opportunity through newly developing and continually improving techniques to help the voter make the proper choice. They also have the opportunity, if they stoop to it, to deceive the voter, to confuse the voter and to increase immeasurably the problems he has in selecting the candidate who most nearly measures up to his standards.

At the turn of the century candidates took to the stump and resorted to the printed word as the only means of getting their messages across.

By the 30s a new dimension had been added—radio.

Then came television and its continuing refinements in techniques—not only the stump speech translated to the small screen, but also the spot announcement, the telethon and similar devices.

Then came the computer and development of personalized direct mail, personalized wires and other methods aimed at making the voter believe the candidate had a direct and personal interest in his well-being.

Primarily these methods are used in an effort, not to inform, but to convince and certainly this is proper.

But our free political system, if it is to survive, depends not so much on a convinced electorate as on an informed electorate. An informed electorate can be convinced on the merits of the case; a properly propagandized electorate may give temporary victory to one party, but the people and the republic lose in the process.

For these reasons, among many, the political parties have growing responsibilities to use the techniques of the new politics—communications techniques, information gathering techniques, attitude determining—honestly and in a manner that benefits the people and the nation.

The press along cannot police the politics of our nation. Government can never be allowed to extend its heavy hand into the right of a candidate or a party to disseminate or collect information or data. Neither can it be allowed to judge the merits of what is disseminated beyond the normal boundaries of libel and slander.

In this area, then, the parties and the politicians and the people must police themselves for their own good and the good of the country.

Otherwise the advancing techniques of the new politics, in the hands of unscrupulous men, can and will be used not to build America but to control it.

We cannot allow that to happen.

—*Robert J. Dole*

"If you are not part of the solution, you are part of the problem."

We at the Republican National Committee have an ambivalent reaction to this modern maxim. We know we are part of the problem and we hope we are part of the solution.

Certainly those of us who are intimately involved in politics (in our society everyone is involved in politics willy-nilly) bear a special responsibility to reappraise our political system.

That reappraisal should commence with a proper appreciation for the attainments of the system: extraordinary mass affluence, exceptional social stability and, most important, remarkable individual freedom.

But these attainments of the system should not blind us to its faults or weaknesses, among which seems to be the sickly state of the two major parties which have been an integral part of that system.

Evidence of this sickness abounds. Fewer people identify with the major parties. The skepticism of adults has been distilled into downright hostility in many young people. Ad hoc groups spring up to champion causes that the major parties seem unwilling or unable to represent effectively. These groups captivate the people and the passions that formerly fired the two-party system.

The causes of the sickness are diverse. They range from the drying up of patronage, the historic glue for our political parties, to the vertiginous acceleration in the pace of our lives that is upsetting our cultural balance and leading to a pervasive feeling of helplessness.

The advent of television and computers has unquestionably contributed to the rapid acceleration in our daily and political lives. Some view the invasion of the political realm by television and computers as sullied evil leading us to ruin. A few even advocate a form of political Luddism that would see us darken the screens and quiet the computers that clack in the mythical smoke-filled rooms.

This attitude is grotesquely unrealistic. Even more, it refuses to recognize the enormous contribution these two technical tools can make toward promoting understanding within the body politic. Both can be extraordinarily effective instruments of communication, and communication is the first way station on the road to understanding.

The new tools supply a way, and we must supply the will to strike at the root of the problem—the decreasing confidence free men have in their ability to govern themselves.

We must make political parties effective engines of

change. We must take the lead in developing and presenting solutions to our pressing problems. We must reach out to involve more people in the political process. For it is only through participation that we can build the confidence our system and our citizenry require.

Beyond this we must understand and have the maturity to accept the limits of politics.

We must understand that not all problems can be solved through the political process. We must understand that those which can be solved can rarely be solved today.

But we must understand that tomorrow is too late to start looking for solutions.

—*Rogers C. B. Morton*

The New Politics and the Old Parties

Finding the People to Match "the Plan"
By Gordon Wade

Humanizing the New Politics
By John G. Stewart

The 1960s confirmed a belief that had been steadily gaining adherents; the Republican and Democratic parties were losing their "clout" with the American electorate at both national and local levels.

In this chapter, two men, a Republican and a Democrat, discuss the reasons for the decline in the importance of their parties. They also outline efforts to revitalize the parties and thus the two-party system, mainstay of politics in the United States.

Both men want to make certain that their national political organizations stay abreast of new techniques for communicating with voters. Both have served as Director of Communications for their respective parties—a job whose complexity has to qualify them as "new politicians."

The first piece is by Gordon Wade formerly of the Republican National Committee; the second by John G. Stewart of the Democratic National Committee.

Finding
the
People
to Match
"the Plan"

by Gordon Wade
former Director of Communications
Republican National Committee

It is both right and wrong to call a political party a constant. Certainly we have had political parties in our country since its inception. They have played a vital role in establishing government. They have helped to express the desires of the electorate; they have helped to focus responsibility and offer alternatives. These are essential elements of governing in a democratic society. However, it is also wrong to call a political party a constant, especially today when both of our national parties are undergoing a period of very rapid change. The basic direction of this change seems to be toward a weakening of their influence. There are several indicators: first, a steady, long-term growth of people who identify themselves as independents. Second, we note in the 1970 elections strong third party senatorial candidates in three states—Connecticut, New York, and Virginia. Of course, two of these three races were won by third party candidates. Additionally, in 1970 we saw an unusually large number of incumbent congressmen defeated in primaries. Practically all of these incumbents had the support of what passed for the local party organization. Yet they were defeated by candidates who built personal organizations.

If you agree that political parties are losing some of their vital force, then it is reasonable to ask why. That question in itself is broad enough to warrant a separate discussion. But I think there are two basic reasons. The first is the decline of patronage, which, in the past, enforced party discipline and provided incentive.With the decline in the amount and appeal of patronage, the parties have been significantly weakened. A second factor contributing to the weakening of our major parties is unquestionably television. Television permits the attractive, well-financed candidate to appeal to broad masses of voters, and weakens the power of local party leadership, which historically has played a major role in critical areas like candidate selection, voter identification, and voter turnout.

In this situation, those of us who believe in the value of political parties have two choices. We can do nothing and allow the parties to slide further into a slough of despondency, or we can attempt to save the party by addressing ourselves to the real problems of present-day organizational politics. We chose the latter course. And we took the approach outlined below.

We analyzed the problems of party organization. In summary they are: poorly defined responsibilities; inadequate or nonexistent goals; poor techniques; poor internal control and monitoring; and rapid, almost constant, turnover of personnel.

In essence, these are the kinds of problems any large business or educational institution might have. If I may draw an analogy, we are talking about a business in which the individual members of a sales force are unclear about the clients on whom they are calling or the products they are selling; do not know how much they are expected to sell; do not know the best way to sell them; have the right to choose their own boss and would prefer not to tell him how well they are not doing the tasks which they are unsure if they should be doing; and can walk off the job at any time because they are volunteers.

This sounds like a formidable set of circumstances to straighten out. And it is. But because we understand the difficulties, we are at least able to approach it in an orderly fashion.

First, we tackled the problem of defining responsibilites using the job description technique employed by American business. We identified all the tasks that needed to be done and assigned them to the different levels of the organization.

Second, we established specific goals or performance standards for each responsibility, again following the techniques of American business.

Third, we collected examples of political techniques from all over the country. We determined the most effective and, at the same time, the most practical techniques and then matched them to the responsibilities and goals. For example, we borrowed a candidate recruitment program from California, a voter turn-out program from Iowa, a fund-raising approach from Indiana.

Fourth, we established a means of monitoring the organization's progress toward the goals established. This was done by developing a comprehensive calendar of all critical events and tying it to a series of forms to be filled out and sent to a central monitoring source.

The final problem—that caused by the constant turnover of volunteer personnel—seemed on the surface to be relatively easy to solve. All we needed to do, we thought, was to put the plan in book form so that it could be handed to the new workers. We felt this would obviate the need to rediscover fire every time a new county chairman or precinct chairman took over.

Unfortunately, this problem was vastly more complex than we had thought, primarily because of the extraordinary diversity in laws and nomenclature across the country. For example, we discovered that a book referring to county chairmen had scant credibility in New England where the local party leader is the town chairman. We soon learned that some states would have jailed local party officials following our original voter turn-out plan. Add to these factors differences in local registration laws—sometimes within the same state—differences in absentee voting requirements, ad infinitum, ad nauseum.

Eventually we came to the conclusion that, in order to attain local credibility, our program would have to be localized for each state. Thanks to modern computerized printing techniques and after several rewrites, we developed the basic manual from which 37 state manuals were written.

Take the Mission 70's manual for the State of Colorado as an example. Without going into excruciating detail, let me share the table of contents with you so you can get a feel for the manual.

The table of contents illustrates the job-description performance-standard approach. The county chairman has five basic responsibilities:

1. To recruit candidates.
2. To build a precinct organization.
3. To implement an action plan.
4. To coordinate the organization.
5. To budget and raise funds.

Within each major area of responsibility, there are individual performance standards to be met. For example, in implementing an action plan, the county chairman has six performance standards to meet:

1. Voter goals.
2. Voter identification.
3. Selective registration.
4. Special ballots.
5. Voter turn-out.
6. Ballot security.

A word about implementation: in 1970, we spent approximately $250,000 taking this program to 37 states. The first step in the implementation was gaining the approval of state leadership to bring the program into the state. Next came a meeting of county chairmen to indoctrinate them. The indoctrination took the form of a three-hour dog and pony show, complete with a film and slide show.

You are entitled to ask what kind of impact this lavish program had upon the 1970 elections. The immediate answer is: we haven't the foggiest notion. We do know the program was not aggressively implemented in Connecticut, in Maryland, or in Tennessee, where our Senate candidates won. We also know that any program as ambitious as this one will take years to implement and reimplement.

The important point is that we have a program that addresses the problems of party organization as we move from the era of patronage politics to the era of participation politics. Now that we have a plan that can work, we have to find people who can work the plan.

Humanizing the New Politics

by John G. Stewart

Director of Communications
Democratic National Committee

What are we likely to remember about the elections of 1970? There are those who argue in behalf of Bob Finch's memorandum outlining the dimensions of the Republican triumph. But I tend to see it a little differently: the elections of 1970 will be remembered for reminding us that the new politics doesn't always win.

I suppose we knew this all along. Only the pundits and analysts who supposedly know about these things kept telling us something else: that the candidate with the professional manager, the polling experts, the computer analysts, the media consultants and film-makers, the sophisticated time-buying specialists couldn't lose. And all it took was money—a lot of money—to guarantee these professional services to any candidate.

27

A year ago the Republican party confidently planned to capture control of the U.S. Senate by arraying these professional campaign services against a host of Democratic incumbents, many of whom appeared to be highly vulnerable. Most of these Democrats won—Burdick, Moss, Hartke, Montoya, Williams, Symington, for example. And because they won, the Democrats are likely to control the Senate for the decade of the 1970's.

It is much too early to know exactly what went wrong, and surely the story will differ from state to state. One should also bear in mind that Albert Gore also lost, a victim—at least in part—of the techniques of the new politics. But this much can be said: on the basis of the 1970 returns, politics would appear to involve more than the latest marketing techniques borrowed from the advertising game, more than the most sophisticated computer programming adapted from the behavioral sciences. Politics still involves candidates, issues, party structure, events, human judgment, and an electorate possessing a remarkable degree of common sense.

I find this revelation quite reassuring.

Now that the faddism of the new politics is perhaps waning, we can get back to the business of trying to understand American politics in all its confounding uncertainty. Much of this book, I assume, will be devoted to precisely this task: sorting out the successes and failures of 1970, trying to place the highly useful techniques of the new politics in some more accurate perspective.

It is now a truism to observe that party loyalty—party identification—is a declining factor for a growing portion of the electorate. The remarkable ticket-splitting in the past election, and in all recent elections, testifies to this fact. But it would be a fatal error to conclude from this that reform of the party's basic structure and procedures is wasted effort.

For nearly 175 years political parties have provided the cement which has held our democratic system together—with the lone exception of the Civil War, the one time in our history when the party system failed. At a time in our history when large segments of our population feel a growing sense of alienation, frustration, and hopelessness, it would appear patently obvious that an invigorated and reformed party structure is desperately needed—for the preservation of our democratic system if for no other reason.

The practitioners of the new politics are proud of their ability to win elections outside the party structure, and they have done so on more than one occasion. But the rest of us should pause a moment, every now and then, to reflect on what happens to the *governmental* process after elections that are won in this fashion. If more and more legislators, if governors and even Presidents, gain public office as men running against the machine—the established party—the governmental process is bound to become more and more fragmented and disjointed. These public officials are likely to assume an increasingly self-centered view of their public responsibilities, in a period when our democratic system can least afford the luxury of such fragmentation.

One need not argue for the maintenance of corrupt and unresponsive political organizations—one need not become an apologist for party loyalty in the parliamentary sense—in order to advocate the urgent need for again taking our political parties seriously: for investing some intellectual energy, some imagination, and even a small amount of money in modernizing our party structure.

We should not expect the professional political managers to close up shop as a patriotic contribution to the preservation of the two-party system. We *should* expect the political parties themselves to modernize their structure and procedures to the extent that people will again come to believe in them as the most effective way to excercise political power, to the extent that the practitioners of the new politics find it in their individual self-interest to operate *within* the party structure rather than outside it. If this is done, the parties will be better off, and so will all the rest of us.

For the past two years at the Democratic National Committee most of our time and energy has been directed toward this end. Of course, we have had no realistic alternative. The techniques of the new politics cost money and this we haven't had. James Perry, authority on the new politics, also tells us that the Republicans have preempted the new technology. And so those of us who came to rest at the Democratic National Committee after the debacle of 1968 had to set our sights in other directions. More than this, we had to look at our party, and our country, and ask this question: What *has* to be done that no one else in the Democratic party can do?

The answers we arrived at reflect some deep feelings and beliefs that have their origins in the closing years of the 1960's. The phenomenon of the Vietnam War, and the rising tide of dissent which sought to express itself through the instrumentality of the Democratic party, suddenly exposed a party structure no longer capable of coping successfully with the nation's major social and political discontents.

These structural problems were there all along. They were not caused by the Vietnam War. Indeed, the bitterly contested struggle at Atlantic City in 1964 over the seating of the Mississippi Freedom Democratic party was a prelude to the disaster in Chicago. The 1964 National Convention laid down the party's first national guidelines on the seating of delegates: future delegations had to be selected by a process open to all interested Democrats, regardless of race. Four years later, in Chicago, the regular Mississippi delegation was thrown out; the challengers, led by Aaron Henry and Charles Evers, were seated. Half the delegates from Georgia were thrown out. And it was decided that a Commission on Party Structure and Delegate Selection—the McGovern Commission—would make a comprehensive study of delegate-selection procedures in all states and recommend necessary reforms so that "all Democratic voters (would have) a full, meaningful and timely opportunity to participate" in the selection of delegates and, thereby, in the decisions of the convention itself.

The McGovern Commission filed its final report last April. Since that time, every state party has been evaluating its delegate-selection procedures; many have already acted on the basis of the guidelines laid down by the McGovern Commission. An ad hoc committee of the National Committee has been appointed to see that the guidelines are implemented by all states for the 1972 National Convention

We can already say with full confidence that the delegates arriving at the '72 convention site will have been selected by a process that is fundamentally open to all persons, of both sexes, of all races, who are 18 years of age or older. And the achievement of this process will have significantly altered the party structure in many states, moving toward a more representative and open structure and away from the more insulated systems which denied effective access to many concerned Democrats in many states.

To us at the Democratic National Committee, we believe this basic overhaul of the party structure and delegate-selection process may be the most effective brand of new politics for the 1970's. And the thrust of these efforts must be toward *humanizing* the party structure.

The 1968 National Convention also created a Rules Commission to modernize the National Convention itself. Under the chairmanship of Representative James O'Hara of Michigan, the Rules Commission is now in the final stages of its work, having devoted the last 18 months to conducting hearings in all sections of the country. Hundreds of Democrats, professors, students, public officials and TV network executives participated.

The objective of the Rules Commission was clear: to establish a set of procedures and a format for the National Convention that strikes the average voter—most likely watching on TV—as *sensible*. The day for horseplay and the suffering of outworn traditions of a pre-television age, hour upon endless hour, has long passed. What takes place inside the convention hall should communicate, at least in some measure, that the political party has some notion of where it is going, some conception of the problems gripping this country, and some believable ideas about how to solve these problems.

Convention business that heretofore interested only the most politically sophisticated observer—credentials and platform issues, for example—are, for many persons, among the most critical issues. What are the rules? How will they be applied? Is everyone getting an equal break? Can the individual delegate make an impact? Is the system fair? Is it *human*?

Those of us who remain too long in Washington tend to be cynical in these matters. But I believe a surprising number of American voters are asking these questions, and waiting in front of their TV sets for some answers.

Thus the Rules Commission attempted to develop procedures which are truly equitable to all concerned in the matter of site selection, arrangements, cost of accommodations, credentials, platform, media coverage, and nominations. And the Rules Commission is creating a format which is attractive, lively, and—above all—*sensible*. This means questioning such well-established institutions as floor demonstrations, favorite son nominations, seconding speeches, the unit rule, and the perfunctory reading of the platform; encouraging such matters as open platform debate on the convention floor and debate among pesidential candidates *before* the balloting begins; and finally, developing a format which sustains a high level of viewer interest from opening to the closing gavel, including scheduling events in such a manner that the critical decisions do not take place at 2:00 A.M. after 85 percent of your audience has collapsed from exhaustion.

If there is any common goal shared by the Democratic National Committee staff, it is the organization of a 1972 National Convention which demonstrates to the American voters in unmistakable terms the rebirth of the party and the readiness of the party to assume national leadership in the White House.

Our efforts of the past two years have gone beyond the problems of the Democratic party itself. The freedom-to-vote task force, under the chairmanship of former Attorney General Ramsey Clark, has investigated the causes of nonvoting and has developed a comprehensive package of legislation to attack this problem, one now approaching critical proportions: 47 million people failed to vote in the 1968 election, an estimated 67 million people stayed home in 1970.

Among other reforms, the task force has proposed a Universal Voter Enrollment Plan, a system that eliminates the diffusion of places and times for registration and places primary responsibility on government to seek out and register voters through a door-to-door canvass, a National Election holiday, and a National Enrollment Commission to supervise the expanded enrollment process. Again, the focus has been toward humanizing the political process, developing procedures that permit individuals to sense their importance in the grand scheme.

Perhaps the time has come for political parties to undertake the contemporary equivalent of the old ward leader's system of personal service, becoming an advocate on consumer issues, for example, or joining forces with public interest groups to protest the despoiling of the environment. We believe this is a pretty sensible brand of new politics. And we believe further that we are way ahead of the Republicans on this score, just as they are ahead of us in the sophisticated use of computers and polling techniques.

There are, of course, other activities at the Democratic National Committee that could be listed under the traditional heading of the new politics:

1. In the fall of 1970 we held the first national political caucus on closed-circuit television: 18 cities interconnected for two hours to discuss issues, campaign techniques, and related matters—all in living color.

2. We are building a computerized data bank of voting statistics, regional socio-economic data, survey research data, and other critical information for use in the 1972 campaign.

3. We are beginning to develop systems for the more productive placement of TV and radio commercials. How can you most effectively reach a particular audience with a message tailored to their concerns? Did you know, for example, that a greater proportion of undecided voters watch the Dick Cavett show than watch Johnny Carson?

4. We are experimenting with many new ways to raise money, from a variety of direct mail appeals to the pilot TV, radio, and newspaper ad campaign we sponsored in three cities this past summer.

5. We have developed a voter identification system that permits volunteers to gather a wealth of information about individual voters and simultaneously perform the task of keypunch operator, vastly reducing operating costs without sacrificing the utility of the data that is collected.

6. We are expanding our in-house radio service that supplies major networks and independent stations with voice actualities on a daily basis, with a specialized weekly service for black, Spanish-speaking, and ethnic stations. We hope to initiate specialized radio programs for college students and housewives.

7. We are exploring ways to develop on audio cassettes a variety of programs that will be used by state and local Democratic groups, everything from issues developed by the Democratic Policy Council to the requirements for delegate selection as set forth by the McGovern Commission.

8. We are continuing our efforts with the networks, the Federal Communications Commission, the federal courts,

and the Congress to develop a more equitable system of political broadcasting, in campaign and non-campaign periods. The existing ground rules are no longer adequate in terms of present circumstances, particularly in those non-campaign periods regulated by the FCC's fairness doctrine.

Our goal in all of this, as I have suggested, is to provide a party structure sufficiently strong and viable to use the techniques of the new politics productively, rather than be destroyed by them. In his volume on the new politics, James Perry concludes with these words:

"Politics once was something akin to good clean fun. It was the great American game, and we could all play it. Sure, it was dirty. And, to be sure, all too often it was dishonest. But it was *human* and it was nonscientific. Now, if the pessimists are right, politics, like so much else, will be dehumanized too. Like Knocko McCormack, most of us will be put on ice."

The elections of 1970 suggested that Perry's pessimists are wrong. Walkin' Lawton Chiles, hiking up and down Florida and spending not a cent on radio and TV commercials, swamped William Cramer, the classic new politician who had everything—polls, computers, slick TV ads, and Vice President Agnew—but lost the election.

We at the Democratic National Committee are putting our money on *humanizing* the politics of the 1970's. If we succeed, there will be ample opportunity to gain maximum benefit from the techniques of the new politics. If we fail, the most sophisticated computer bank in the Western hemisphere won't save us.

A Look
at the
New
Techniques

Zeroing in on the Voter
By Joseph Napolitan

Balancing the Campaign
By F. Clifton White

Taking the Voter's Pulse
By Walter DeVries

What Really Happened in 1970
By Richard M. Scammon

In this section, four outstanding political experts tell what they did and how they assess its value in the 1970 campaign. Three of these experts are campaign handlers—political consultants who plan and manage election campaigns for the politicians. The fourth expert is one of the world's leading campaign and election watchers and analysts.

Joseph Napolitan, first president of the American Association of Political Consultants, is considered to be the foremost new political campaign handler. He guided Hubert Humphrey's presidential campaign in 1968, and has worked for leading congressional and gubernatorial candidates, including Governor Burns of Hawaii, Governor Mandel of Maryland, and Governor Shapp of Pennsylvania (whose rise from political obscurity was directed by Napolitan in the classic example of the use of money and television as tools of the new politics).

F. Clifton White, current president of the American Association of Political Consultants, is Napolitan's alter ego.

While Napolitan handles only liberal candidates, White works only for conservatives, but both have been closely associated with the development of an organization for political consultants. White's supreme victory was his management of the campaign of conservative James L. Buckley for the U.S. Senate from New York in 1970. White was manager for Senator Barry Goldwater's presidential campaign in 1964, and has worked for leading conservatives at all political levels.

Dr. Walter DeVries has also played an important role in the formation and operation of the American Association of Political Consultants. While Napolitan and White are the craftsmen of the new politics, DeVries is the scientist. He is a professor of political science at the University of Michigan, and has long been an advocate of using the techniques of the social sciences in politics. He has handled Republican politics in Michigan for such candidates as Governor Milliken, former Governor Romney, and senatorial candidate Lenore Romney.

Finally, Richard M. Scammon brings to this section his own perceptive analysis of the true facts of the 1970 campaign. It was his book, *The Real Majority* (written with co-author Ben Wattenberg), which was the big political book of the year. Every politician had to read it, and its basic thesis— that the American voter is a middle-of-the-roader—influenced almost every campaign in the country. Scammon has been a political election watcher as director of the Elections Research Center in Washington, D.C. since 1955, with four years off to serve as Director of the Census. He is also editor of the *America Votes* series, *America at the Polls*, co-author of *This U.S.A.* and a consultant for NBC News Election coverage.

39

Looking at the overall results of the 1970 elections, it should be pointed out here that not all those who practiced the new politics were winners. Indeed, the 1970 elections were seen as a test of the new politics; and when it was over some analysts, such as Bernard Nossiter of the *Washington Post*, wrote that the voters had "blurred the image of the TV image makers."

Nossiter prepared a box score of some of the new political consultants, showing that they lost almost as often as they won.

Image Makers' Record

Joseph Napolitan (D) 3-1 (winners, losers).
>   Winners: Burns, Gov., Hawaii; Mandel, Gov., Md;
>   Licht, Gov., R.I.
>   Loser: White, Gov., Mass.

Roger Ailes (R) 2-2
>   Winners: Meskill, Gov., Conn.; Sargent, Gov., Mass.
>   Loser: Olson, Gov., Wis.; Roudebush, Sen., Ind.

David Garth (D) 3-3
>   Winners: Stevenson, Sen., Ill.; Gilligan, Gov., Ohio;
>   Tunney, Sen., Calif.
>   Losers: Ottinger, Sen., N.Y.; Walinsky, Atty. Gen.,
>   N.Y.; DeSimone (R), Gov., R.I.

Charles Guggenheim (D) 4-3
>   Winners: Hart, Sen., Mich.; Lucey, Gov., Wis.;
>   Kennedy, Sen., Mass.; Moss, Sen., Utah.
>   Losers: Gore, Sen., Tenn.; Metzenbaum, Sen.,
>   Ohio; Duffey, Sen., Conn.

Harry Treleaven (R) 1-4
    Winners: Brock, Sen., Tenn.
    Losers: Bush, Sen., Texas; Romney, Sen., Mich.;
        Kleppe, Sen., N.Dak.; Cramer, Sen., Fla.
Totals—13 winners, 13 losers.

Of course, not all new political consultants are represented in Nossiter's analysis. Among those not mentioned
were two of our own representatives in this section, White
and DeVries, both of whom were winners with Senator Buckley in New York and Governor Milliken in Michigan, respec-
tively.

Whether winners or losers, all politicians are spending
much more money on political campaigning, primarily because of the need for new political techniques, particularly
television advertising and computer help. Campaign costs
have become so enormous that this itself is one of the major
issues in any discussion of the new politics. Much legislation
has been proposed to curb or limit campaign spending. One
bill passed by Congress to limit the amount of money that
could be spent on television was vetoed by President Nixon
just a few weeks before the November 1970 elections.

Most new political consultants themselves agree to limitations on campaign spending. The American Association of
Political Consultants passed a post-election resolution calling
on Congress to override the President's veto. In part, the
resolution said: "We agree with the President that the problem of reducing campaign broadcast spending represents only
a part of the overall problem of electoral reform, but it is an
important first step toward reducing costs of campaigns and

41

assuring an electoral system which guarantees that candidates will have equal access to the airwaves."

Increasingly, the cost of campaigning has made politics a rich man's business. In the 1968 presidential election year, political expenditures were estimated at $300 million. Almost $60 million was spent for air-time for television and radio spots, and production of those spots is estimated to have cost another $30 million.

In the non-presidential 1970 campaign, the costs may go even higher, when the final count is complete, because the services of specialists, orchestrating generalists, and advertising time and space have all gone up in price, according to the Citizens' Research Foundation at Princeton, N.J., which has been studying the problem.

An analysis of campaign spending in the 1970 election by the *Washington Post* (Table II-1) showed that almost every candidate spent more money on broadcast time than the new law would have allowed, and all these sums were exorbitant.

Table II-1. BROADCAST SPENDING

STATE	CANDIDATE	Estimate of Amt. Spent in 1970* for general election	Amt. permissible under proposed law for the general election
California	John Tunney (D)	$ 800,000.00 **	$497,172.55
	George Murphy (R)	$ 500,000.00	$497,172.55
Florida	Lawton M. Chiles, Jr. (D)	$ 30,000.00	$141,689.52
	William C. Cramer (R)	not filed	$141,689.52
Illinois	Adlai Stevenson III (D)	$ 314,000.00	$311,481.17
	Ralph T. Smith (R)	$ 305,000.00	$311,481.17
Indiana	Vance Hartke (D)	$ 246,000.00	$143,718.26
	Richard L. Roudebush (R)	$ 441,000.00	$143,718.26
Maryland	Joseph D. Tydings (D)	$ 55,111.00 ***	$ 79,360.89
	J. Glenn Beall, Jr. (R)	$ 92,533.00 ***	$ 79,360.89

(*Continued*)

42

Table II-1. (Cont'd.)

STATE	CANDIDATE	Estimate of Amt. Spent in 1970 * for general election	Amt. permissible under proposed law for the general election
Minnesota	Hubert H. Humphrey (D)	$ 223,000.00	$111,195.70
	Clark MacGregor (R)	$ 220,000.00	$111,195.70
New York	Richard Ottinger (D)	$1,000,000.00	$460,711.09
	James Buckley (C)	$ 500,000.00	$460,711.09
	Charles Goodell (R)	$ 700,000.00	$460,711.09
N. Dakota	Quentin N. Burdick (D)	$ 49,949.00	$ 20,000.00
	Thomas S. Kleppe (R)	$ 69,343.00	$ 20,000.00
Tennessee	Albert Gore (D)	$ 150,000.00	$ 87,403.05
	William E. Brock III (R)	$ 250,000.00	$ 87,403.05
Texas	Lloyd M. Bentsen, Jr. (D)	not available	$204,144.64
	George Bush (R)	not available	$204,144.64

* Includes 15% advertising agency fee

** Includes the primary election

*** Does not include radio spending

In Table II-2, from the *Washington Post*, the total campaign spending of these candidates, illustrating the high cost of politics in the age of the new politics, is shown:

Table II-2. CAMPAIGN SPENDING

STATE	CANDIDATE	Estimate of Campaign Spending	Expenditures Reported to Secy. of Senate as of Oct. 24
California	John Tunney (D)	$1,600,000	—0—
	George Murphy (R)	$1,500,000	$ 757,353.61
Florida	Lawton M. Chiles, Jr. (D)	$ 350,000	$ 11,600.90
	William C. Cramer (R)	$ 547,000	—0—
Illinois	Adlai Stevenson III (D)	$ 950,000	$ 25,120.00
	Ralph T. Smith (R)	$1,100,000	—0—
Indiana	Vance Hartke (D)	$ 550,000	—0—
	Richard L. Roudebush (R)	$1,000,000	—0—
Maryland	Joseph D. Tydings (D)	$ 500,000	—0—
	J. Glenn Beall, Jr. (R)	$ 425,000	$ 10,200.00
Minnesota	Hubert H. Humphrey (D)	$550,000-$600,000	$ 300.00
	Clark MacGregor (R)	$550,000-$600,000	$ 1,625.95

(Continued)

43

Table II-2. (Cont'd.)

STATE	CANDIDATE	Estimate of Campaign Spending	Expenditures Reported to Secy. of Senate as of Oct. 24
New York	Richard Ottinger (D)	$2,000,000	$ 24,325.55
	James Buckley (C)	$2,000,000	$1,141,377.92
	Charles Goodell (R)	$1,300,000	$ 232,983.25
N. Dakota	Quentin N. Burdick (D)	$100,000-$150,000	$ 300.00
	Thomas S. Kleppe (R)	$280,000-$300,000	$ 1,300.00
Tennessee	Albert Gore (D)	$ 500,000	$ 2,418.84
	William E. Brock III (R)	$1,000,000	$ 26,110.06
Texas	Lloyd M. Bentsen, Jr. (D)	$1,031,912	—0—
	George Bush (R)	$ 991,292	$ 8,193.33

NOTE: Candidates are only required to report their expenditures for the general election, though some reports contain primary spending as well.

There is little doubt that some legislation will be passed before 1972 that will have an affect on political campaign spending. But there is also little doubt that the principles and techniques described in this section by three political consultants, and the analysis of the electorate described here by Richard Scammon, will continue to be important in the planning and organizing of the 1972 campaigns.

Zeroing in on the Voter

by Joseph Napolitan
President
Joseph Napolitan Associates, Inc.

I am going to describe eight or nine new techniques that we used this year. They may not really be "new" techniques but only improvements. I don't really think that there is very much new in politics. Maybe we refined someone else's idea. Sometimes what we think is new in one state may have been used twelve years in another state. But here are some things that either we used for the first time this year or we used with a little different twist.

One of the very simple ones was making the disclaimer on radio and television spots part of the message. How did we do this? We formed a committee in several states, for example, Massachusetts, which is where we first used it. There the committee was called "A Lot of People Who Want to See Kevin White Elected Governor," which meant exactly what it said: that all of our political television or radio spots were sponsored by "a lot of people who wanted Kevin White elected governor." And, as a matter of fact, we went a step further and said, "And *that's* why this message has been brought to you by a lot of people who want to see Kevin White elected Governor." He wasn't elected, incidentally, but we did use this technique successfully in three or four other states.

We take a lot for granted. We knew we had this disclaimer, but somebody came up with the idea of utilizing it, making it a part of the message, incorporating it in with everything else. We could even do this on ten-second spots. "Joe Jones is honest and that's why this message is brought to you by a lot of people who want to see Jones elected governor." The disclaimer takes seven seconds of the ten-second message, but it makes a point.

This year we made some changes in the political time-buying curve. Traditionally, we've used a reasonably standard formula for political time-buying. You spend a sixth of your money in the third week before the election, a third of it in the second week, and a half of it in the final week. So you just accelerate to the end. In some campaigns this year we tried something we called the spurt technique. We would go on television very early, maybe as early as March or April in some cases, with an intensive week or ten days at a selected period. You look good on television or radio at a time when there is no one else on the air waves and you've got it all to yourself. Maybe we would run a week of television, then go off completely; or run a week of radio, then go off completely; or come back with a week of television. The audience gets the feeling that you're on all the time. But you're only laying the ground work, and it can work most effectively.

In Hawaii we used this technique to very good advantage. We did a campaign for Governor John Burns, who was running for reelection. Hawaii has the latest primary in the country, on October 3rd, just exactly a month before the general election. Our first poll for Burns, which was taken in December 1969, a year ago, showed him trailing his Democratic lieutenant governor in the primary by sixteen points. There weren't many undecided voters, so the opposition had a pretty solid lead at the time.

We concocted three separate groups of television spots which we actually used twice each. The first group was spots devoted entirely to Governor Burns' record in office. We found out that people had no idea what he had done. He had been governor for eight years, but the population of Hawaii is so fluid that people had not lived there long enough to know his record. So we made a batch of television spots simply on his record. He didn't appear in any of them; they didn't ask people to vote for Burns. The concluding message was very simple. It asked people to think about Burns and what he had done. Four or five spots in each batch; all were either 30- or 60-second spots. We ran those very early in March and April. We went on the air with them a couple of weeks, went off for a couple of weeks, and we went back on for a week or so.

A second batch of spots was based partly on his accomplishments, but for the first time we introduced Burns into the material as well. Some were in stills and some were in film. He did not speak in any of these, but he was shown while a voice spoke. We ran two spurts of this second wave of spots.

47

The third wave of spots were tied in with a half-hour documentary film. These all ran solidly straight through in the last three weeks of the campaign. This third wave was all on Burns the man. He spoke; he was active; he was out campaigning. He looked as well as he could. The problem in Hawaii was that John Burns was an old, unattractive, inarticulate man running against a younger, attractive, articulate opponent. Even on the day of the primary the newspapers said the race was too close to call. They couldn't tell who was ahead. Burns received 54 percent of the vote to 46—a really solid victory and an example of how the spurt technique was effectively used in a particular campaign.

Another technique used in some campaigns this year we call "instant information." Frankly, I don't think we used it enough, and I think it is one of the techniques that will be used much more frequently in elections from now on. In a speech he made a few years ago, Marshall McLuhan said, "Instant information creates involvement." What we do is capitalize on current events. Radio spots, particularly, are used because they can be produced very quickly; and in some cases television spots are produced overnight to capitalize on a situation.

Let me give you a couple of examples of how these instantly produced radio spots can work. We had a situation at a hearing in Alaska in a campaign we did up there in the spring. At the hearing in the state house in Juneau the spokesman for one of the candidates for governor made a statement that we thought was weak, on which we could capitalize. I sat down and wrote a 60-second radio spot on a yellow pad, telephoned to Anchorage, and dictated it to a secretary. She got it to an announcer, who read it, and tape recorded it. They fed it back by a radio wire we had hooked up to all the radio stations in Alaska. This was at five o'clock in the afternoon. On the way back to the airport the next morning, I heard the spot on radio in Juneau. Fourteen hours from the time the statement was made, I heard our spot on the radio; that is pretty fast work.

The same situation arose in another election this year. When the governor we were running against made a statement that we felt was weak, we came right back and got it on the air immediately. We also found in Massachusetts that the technique was being used against us. The Republican governor and his people had picked up the idea and were using the same technique we were using.

I think you'll find this technique used frequently in future campaigns, and I think that it will be used on television as well as on radio. You'll find candidates with time allocated so they can go in at the last minute, make a statement very quickly, and get it on the air. They can capitalize not only on what opponents or others in the race may say but on any natural disasters or important news. If the subway fares in New York City go up, a candidate can get on television immediately and make a comment. This is in addition to news. These are paid spots. But they are in news style. They say almost exactly the same thing as a news spot, and maybe they are the same thing, except you pay to get your message on the air. You reinforce it and get it on more often than a news spot would get on.

The telenews technique is something else that I think we are going to see more of. It was used more this year than it has ever been used before. Using this procedure you make sure that your candidate gets on the news programs by taking the responsibility of providing stations throughout the state with video tape or film or radio tape of what he says and what he does. This has been done on radio for a long while. For five or six years—a long while in this business—we have had a man follow a candidate around with a tape recorder. He calls 84 radio stations and says, "I've got candidate X speaking to the State Druggists' Association this morning, and I've got thirty-seven seconds of what he said. Would you like it?" The station is 140 miles away, didn't send anybody to cover the meeting, and sure they'd be glad to take it. And you get about a 90 percent response. Now we're having more such events filmed, having a crew around especially when you know the candidate is going to be making a reasonably newsworthy statement or going to be at a reasonably newsworthy event. We immediately process our material and ship it to television stations all over the state. We give them a piece of film or tape instead of a mimeographed press release. Obviously, it works out better. The candidate gets more exposure, and the chances of getting it used are much better.

Polling techniques are also changing. In addition to our basic polling techniques we've gone much deeper than we ever did before into trying to find out the reasons why people vote. And I'm not sure anybody really knows why anybody votes for anybody. We have also come up with a series of almost continuous polls, straw vote polls, and weekly polls that don't do anything except measure changes in attitudes either on voting patterns, voting intentions, or one or two simple issues. We have found this works most successfully if we establish the program, give it professional direction and guidance, but let the campaign organization staff it. One or two bright people can set it up.

They might use telephone polls, or straw vote polls, or shopping center polls. These are good only to determine changes. Obviously, you're not going to predict the outcome of an election by taking polls at a shopping center. But if you poll the same shopping center for twelve consecutive Saturdays, reaching basically the same type of people who go there week after week, you're going to detect changes or shifts in attitudes or intentions. You can measure this if you know that you've started your television on the week of September 15th, and suddenly you're up four points in the polls; and you intensify your television a little bit, and you go up another two or three points. You can assume that your television is having some effect. If it goes the other way, maybe you ought to go back to newspaper advertising.

Another change is that we're mixing our media better. We recognize the importance and potency of television, but we're also learning that in some areas, with some special groups, radio is more effective; with some groups newspaper advertising is more effective. If we've got a message for women, we not only try to get to women through television programs in the afternoon, but we might also prepare a newspaper ad and run it on the social page. If we have an ad that appeals to men, we might try to play it before a football game on Sunday afternoon, but we might also buy a print ad in the sports section or buy some radio time after the sports broadcast. So we are becoming more selective in targeting the audience.

We are further recognizing that issues are not really as important as the impressions that people make. In a campaign in Alaska this spring, we lost the primary. We did a post-primary poll and we asked questions like, "Whose tele-

vision spots do you see the most? Who was best on television?" "Larry Carr." "Whose radio spots did you hear the most?" "Carr." "Who was best on radio?" "Carr." "Who brought up the best issues in the campaign?" "Carr." "Who did you vote for?" "Egan." When we tried to analyze and go a little deeper, we found out that it was not the issues in the campaign, it was just the general impressions left by the men. We recently completed a poll in which we asked this question: "If you see a half hour film about a candidate, what do you want to feel about that candidate after you have seen the film?" Forty-seven percent of the people said they wanted to feel that the man was honest; 16 percent said they wanted to feel that he was capable; nothing else scored higher than 8 percent. Issues were down to about 4 percent. In other polls we asked questions like, "Which is more important to you, that a candidate in this election has a position on the issues very similiar to your own or that he is able to cope with situations that may arise?" It was 74 to 14 in favor of coping with situations as they arise. I think everybody in the business has known this, but we are beginning to probe it a little better.

Just one other point: I think campaigns and candidates are learning how to use professionals better. Not only are there generalists in the business, but there are others who are experts in a very narrow sphere of political communication; it might be something like *lighting* the candidate or counseling a candidate about how he should act on television. There are any number of these very narrow areas. Instead of trying to use a man just because he has worked in the mail room for the party for the last 18 years, it may be better to hire a $500-a-day man to set up your computerized letters. We find that we are doing this effectively in campaigns in which we get involved. Rather than letting people do it because they've been around and they're nice people, we get the best person we can find. These are expensive people, but they really don't cost that much; if they're any good, they will usually save us money in the long run. And we hire them for very short periods. We've worked in campaigns where we hire a television consultant to advise a candidate for two or three days. Maybe it's $1,000 or $1,500, but it's money well spent. And by selecting the people and knowing who the good people are, campaigns are both improving the quality of their political messages and, I think, being run more economically in the long run.

Balancing the Campaign

by F. Clifton White
President
F. Clifton White & Associates, Inc.

First, I am not sure there is anything new in politics. Second, I am very much concerned that a large number of us involved in campaigning today, to some extent, have become so involved in the techniques that we forget the objectives of the campaign. We have developed some reasonably sophisticated techniques, which are not always effective in terms of the overall objective of the campaign itself.

Obviously, the one medium that everyone has become intrigued with is television. But I would hope that candidates have not succumbed to a belief that by getting on television they can win an election. There are some great experts around the country who will testify that it is possible to lose an election by getting on television too much just as easily as it is to win an election that way.

I think we may very well have seen the maximum use of television in the 1970 elections. This was one of those years when everybody came out and said television is the answer and all we've got to do is to get a whole bunch of tape and buy some time and we'll get elected. But it isn't necessarily so.

Sure, we have developed some new techniques, but the fundamental principles of political campaigning really are not new. We make a serious error, and quite frequently may lose an election, when we get too intrigued with one aspect of the campaign to the detriment of the rest. I think this happened a good deal in 1970, especially with regard to television.

The objective of any campaign, of course, is to get more votes for our candidate than the other manager gets for his, at that given moment in time when a voter has an opportunity to cast a ballot. We have a wide constituency in almost any election—congressional, senatorial, gubernatorial, and, of course, presidential. All of us know from the data that we have about this wide constituency that there is a variety of methods for communicating with the voter. And we achieve success in a campaign when we establish the appropriate blend of those instruments available for communicating with this wide constituency. This includes not only the electronic media but also the print media. It also includes the organizational effort, the one to one, the personal friend, the conversation, to reach the maximum number of people with a predisposition toward the candidate by virtue of party affiliation, personality, position on issues, or the ability to get people in that constituency in some way or another to identify with him.

As many know, I am very strong on a great deal of lead time in any campaign. Sometimes this is difficult for a professional manager to achieve because often candidates do not hire a professional manager until they are convinced they are going to be serious candidates. But I believe that we can first run the most effective campaign, and second, utilize all the techniques that are available when we have time to plan the campaign. I think a good deal of disaster occurs in campaigns that are planned in late September and early October. I am convinced that total disaster occurs when the planning is done the last week of October.

We ought to be able to sit down and use what is called the new politics or the new techniques—the tools and the information that are available—very early in a campaign: get basic facts, determine the constituency, determine the people available, and form polling techniques from polling information. Find out who those people are, and find out those vehicles available for communicating with them. Develop a thrust, establish a campaign plan, and by Labor Day at the latest, we ought to have a plan of how to use the total effort for the 67 or 68 days of a particular campaign effort. Time and money spent at this time will save you large amounts of money later in the campaign.

Secondly, there always has to be a degree of flexibility in the planning because it is never certain how much money you are going to have and how effectively, therefore, you will be able to implement your plan. A total blend of techniques are needed in a campaign. Quite frequently we prepare our budgets and put in what we think we need for television and what we think we need for print media. We start buying television, but then if we don't get the money, we suddenly find we don't have the money for print or radio or for the organizational effort. As a result we end up not with a well-balanced campaign plan but with an erratic one.

I would emphasize and underline that a well-balanced campaign is really what wins the election. Even if it never achieves the maximum, if it is well balanced and well blended from the beginning, the opportunities for success are greater than if we run an erratic campaign.

One of the connotations of the new politics is that the old kind of political organization no longer has the influence or impact in the electoral process that many of us thought it had historically. To an extent this is true, but I don't believe it is true when it comes to organization. I still believe that if you are going to have effective politics, new or old, it is extremely important to have the kind of organization where candidates communicate with their constituency as people.

What may be new, and in my judgment increasingly critical in the 1970's, is that we are probably going to have to build our own local organization. The traditional political party organization follows a pattern of contact with the constituency, thereby frequently ignoring a potential block of supporters and voters because of heritage and tradition. We are living in a period of politics with significant shifts in voting behavior patterns. The reasons why people voted the way they did historically has been the subject of many classical studies. These may have been valid at the time, but most, I believe, are not valid today. People are changing.

Political scientists and social psychologists might do some research and give us more information on this, but from a casual observation of history, this phenomenon of change appears to have occurred four or five times in our history. From 1824 to 1828 there was a significant voting behavior change among the population that resulted in the dominance of one party for a period of 20 to 30 years. This happened again from 1854 to 1860 and from 1932 to 1940. I think it is occurring again. This is significant, it seems to me, in terms of political organization.

It was significant in terms of the victory of the conservative candidate, James Buckley, in the senatorial election in New York state in 1970. Maybe this race wasn't completely typical because there were three candidates, but I do think the new organizational principle applied. We had to establish our own independent organization. This wasn't the old phony sort of thing where we found someone enrolled as a Democrat and prevailed upon him to head up something called "Democrats for Your Candidate." This was a realistic organization which appealed to a variety of people prepared to and interested in shifting their voting behavior. It included Democrats; it included Republicans; it included independents and conservatives. In another breakdown, it included the ethnic groups: Italians, Poles, Lithuanians, Germans, or whatever. In another breakdown, according to jobs, it included labor union members, farmers, and many others. It was an organization that appealed to these people and blended them into one single body which gave communication across the board to all their objectives and ended up with their vote. Many Democrats felt that their mistake, or misjudgment, was the Democratic vote the conservatives received in New York City, which was exceedingly high by most historical standards. It wasn't high if we look at some of the shifting voting behavior patterns that had been occurring in New York City. Interestingly enough Mayor Lindsay's election, which showed some discernible shifts, gave us evidence of new groupings that we could talk to and organize for Jim Buckley.

One aspect of the new politics that is important—and I'm not sure how well any of us have learned to deal with it—is the news show, both on television and radio. People have apparently established new listening and viewing habits. They get their news at either 6:30, 7:30, or 10 o'clock. This has become a habit; they listen to one station, and they aren't going to tune us out if we are on that particular news show at that particular hour. They'll listen to us; they'll hear us; or they'll see us. It is not the easiest thing in the world, but campaign managers must consciously plan to make appearances on news shows.

Here again, we can use our new techniques to influence our constituency. We know which constituency tends to watch what kind of television or radio news show. If we have determined our constituency—where our potential votes are—then we have to consciously plan to have our candidate and our programs presented on that particular type of show, wherever it may be.

This is not easy, of course. The people who run those shows are constantly alerted to our schemes. For example, in the state of New York one cannot under any circumstances have a candidate spend seven or eight days in upstate New York. He will never appear on the New York City news shows if he does. They don't send anybody to cover upstate. We might be seen on an upstate station occasionally because of a network news show, but it never works the other way around. So we have to plan our campaign to make sure that our candidate is never out of the city for more than three or three-and-a-half days at a time. We have to get him back into town to do something—where those six or seven channels and cameras are—so that if we can make them believe something our candidate is doing is newsworthy, they will cover us. Then we get on all channels, across the board. This kind of exposure is important in the new politics.

Lastly, because of the instantaneous nature of television, we have to be prepared to take advantage of events. We can do everything I have suggested up to this point; we can have the best plan in the world; but an event taking place at any juncture in our campaign can have an impact on the voters because it will be in their living rooms that evening. Everyone will be taken up with it; if it is an emotional event they will become emotionally involved. Our candidate had better be identified with that concern in the voters' minds. Quite frequently an identification of candidate with event can move the candidate 30 points in a poll within 12 hours. People emotionally involved with an event, finding a man in the public eye sharing that concern, are apt to say, "Boy, we've got to do something, and here is the guy who can do it. He was there and he understood it. He is as concerned as I am, and he wants to do something about it, and we'd better get him into office just as quickly as we can."

Obviously, this is not the sort of thing we can plan. But we had better be prepared in our planning of the campaign to take advantage of any such events that may transpire. Otherwise, we'll be devastated by an event over which we had no control but which really captured the imagination of the people, one with which they became emotionally involved and concerned one way or another.

As I said in the beginning, I'm not sure there is much that is new in politics. We have some new techniques. But I would underline my deep feeling that in running a political campaign, the objective is to communicate to constituents and to persuade the majority of them to support us. Doing this effectively requires the utilization of all the techniques available, not just one or two new gimmicks.

Taking the Voter's Pulse

by Walter DeVries, *Professor,*
University of Michigan, and
Senior Consultant, DeVries and Associates

Assessments of the effectiveness of campaign techniques suffer from two problems. If you won the election, the techniques were obviously effective. But if you lost the election, it was because your opponent manipulated the techniques and conned the electorate into some irrational behavior.

In dealing with my topic, I want to refer to data that we've worked on in Michigan since 1962, and in particular the polls and other studies done from January 1969 through November 16, 1971. I believe—from my work in other states—that you can generalize from the Michigan experiences to a good many other states. Today, then, we use Michigan as a case study.

A few background notes about the results of the 1970 Michigan election: Governor William Milliken was one of only two Midwestern Republican governors who won in 1970. He received 50.7 percent of the vote. For most state-wide offices (*e.g.*, U.S. senator, secretary of state, attorney general) the average Republican vote was slightly over 40 percent. There were three constitutional amendments on the ballot as well. The first dealt with a hundred million dollar low-income housing bond issue. The Governor strongly supported this proposal. It lost 60-40. The second proposal on the ballot was the 18-year-old vote. The Governor also strongly supported this. It lost 60-40. The third proposal prohibited aid to nonpublic schools. The Governor opposed the passage of that amendment. It carried about 60-40. In terms of both the Republican statewide candidates on the ballot and the issues, the vote was about 60-40 against Governor Milliken.

I did a post-election study on November 16 to determine how the undecided voters had moved in the last five to seven days before the election. I also did some spot checks of the voting behavior in the gubernatorial contest. I told the Governor that, based on these findings, it was impossible for us to have won that election.

Let me say, parenthetically, in response to an attack on the new politics, that I am a true believer in the practice of the communications techniques that characterize the new politics. I believe anything that makes campaign strategies correspond with political reality is good for democratic systems. I don't believe that political campaigns have to be irrelevant and inconsiderate of the concerns of the voters. I find nothing Machiavellian about asking what problems bother people, or asking what they think ought to be done about these problems. Once I find that out, I don't think it Machiavellian to find the best media to inform people what the candidate intends to do or not do about these problems, or why he is better able to handle them than his opponent.

The techniques of the new politics have succeeded only because the two traditional political parties have failed. The parties have not really reformed the nomination or general election processes, and the voters know it. The new politics are a service to this republic—not a disservice. By better communicating with voters, these practitioners have helped raise information levels about American politics and government. This has increased the confidence and ability of the voter to judge more accurately parties and candidates. This, of course, has resulted in more and more ticket-splitting. This concerns the party professionals—and academics who professionally worry about this sort of thing—because they don't understand this and therefore resent it. It also, I might add, piques certain members of the press because they suspect that some of the practitioners of the new politics know better how to communicate with voters than they do.

That ends my polemic about the new politics—which is really nothing more than good communications between candidates and voters.

To return to my post-election study, the context of my observations and findings is this:

The ideal (perfect) way to campaign (or govern) is to have a near flawless, up-to-date, two-way communications system between the candidates and the voters and the capability to respond to the information inputs in the system. The best (*i.e.*, efficient) campaign then allocates resources—money, time, and energy— to meet your communications objectives.

In short, I see campaigning (and governing) as an information and communications system.

The tables I am now distributing to you range from the simplistic to the unintelligible.

Table II-3 depicts some of the general trends in competitive statewide races in general election contests. With a few southern exceptions, the states in this nation are now competitive. I am referring principally to races for governor, the U.S. Senate and, of course, the presidential contest.

Today when you ask people how they make up their minds about candidates, you get the kind of responses that are listed in the left-hand column in Table II-3—the candidate's ability to handle the job, personality, his stand on issues, party affiliation, and so on. This rank order was not true 20 or 30 years ago, and, indeed, some of my colleagues still believe that people make up their minds on the basis of party first, then group affiliations, candidates, and issues. This chart emphasizes the continued decrease of party influence and the increase of importance in the candidate's ability to handle the job and his stand on issues.

Table II-4 is based on an open-ended question to 809 Michigan voters on how they make up their minds in deciding political matters. All voting groups (behavioral Republicans, behavioral Democrats, and ticket-splitters) are included. Parenthetically, I should point out that I do not use self-identification as a way of labeling Democrats, Republicans, and independents. My only measurement for "independence" is the splitting of the ticket. So the voters in these tables are labeled behavioral (*i.e.*, straight) Republicans, Democrats, and ticket-splitters.

Note in Table II-4 that the responses we received were

principally clustered about candidates—their personality and background and ability to do the job. The way people perceive the candidate—in competitive statewide general elections—is not the most important variable in voting behavior.

Table II-5 shows that voters get their information about candidates and issues from a variety of media. I define a medium as any instrument that conducts information, whether it be family, friends, television, radio, or organizations.

Two-thirds of the variables cited as most important in voter decision-making related to candidates. These factors were seen as twice as important as issues. Party and media responses were seen at quite similar but low levels of importance.

Of course, as you will see, the voters get this information about candidates, issues, and parties from a variety of media.

We asked voters to examine a list of 36 variables that might have some impact on the way they made up their minds about political matters. They then rated each one of these variables on an 11-point scale. The results are rank ordered from most to least important by two voting groups—undecided voters in the 1970 gubernatorial contest and ticket-splitters.

Take a look at all of the variables that are rated about five points. Among the interpersonal media you have family and candidates. Among the audio-visual media, the first five variables are all above five points. Among the audio media, only radio educational programs and radio newscasts are above five points. Among the print media, only newspaper editorials and newspaper stories are over the five-point mark. In the organizational category only the Democratic party had a five-point rating.

Table II-3. HOW VOTERS MAKE UP THEIR MINDS
ABOUT CANDIDATES

TODAY .... *and* .... *NOT SO LONG AGO*

1. *Candidates*   1. *Party*
   ability to handle the job
   personality

2. *Issues*   2. *Group Affiliations*
   candidates' stands
   candidates' and party's ability to
      handle problems

3. *Party*   3. *Candidates*
   identification
   membership

4. *Group Affiliations*   4. *Issues*
   religious
   ethnic
   occupational

Table II-4. MOST IMPORTANT THINGS
IN DECIDING POLITICAL MATTERS *
(Michigan, May 1970; n = 809)

Candidate-oriented responses:
    Personality and background 48.1%
    Ability to do the job 28.0
    Stand on issues 19.9

Issue-oriented responses: 36.8

Party-oriented responses: 11.9

Media-oriented responses: 9.5

Others/Don't know 15.2
(multiple responses)

* The question asked was: "As you make up your mind about political matters, what are the most important things that come to mind?"

Reproduced with the permission of Governor William G. Milliken.

Table II-5. RELATIVE IMPORTANCE OF FACTORS THAT INFLUENCE THE VOTING DECISIONS OF 1970 GUBERNATORIAL UNDECIDED *
(May 1970; n = 809)

MEDIA	1970 Gubernatorial undecided	Ticket-splitters
Interpersonal		
Talks with family	5.5	5.6
Contacts with candidates	5.0	5.2
Talks with friends	4.8	5.0
Talks with political party workers	4.3	4.2
Talks with work associates	4.3	4.3
Talks with neighbors	3.8	3.9
Audiovisual		
Television newscasts	6.7	6.8
Television documentaries and specials	6.5	6.6
Television editorials	5.7	5.6
Television talk shows	5.6	5.6
Television educational programs	5.6	5.9
Television advertisements	3.6	3.6
Television entertainers	2.6	2.5
Movies	1.8	1.8
Stage plays	1.4	1.4
Audio		
Radio educational programs	5.3	5.5
Radio newscasts	5.3	5.5
Radio talk shows	4.5	4.9
Radio editorials	4.2	4.5
Radio advertisements	3.0	3.0
Telephone campaign messages	2.3	2.0
Phonograph records	1.3	1.1
Print		
Newspaper editorials	5.8	5.9
Newspaper stories	5.8	6.0
Magazine editorials	4.3	4.2
Political brochures	3.8	3.6
Magazine stories	3.8	4.0
Newspaper advertisements	3.8	3.7

(*Continued*)

Table II-5. (Cont'd.) MEDIA	1970 Gubernatorial undecided	Ticket-splitters
Books	3.6	3.6
Political mailings	3.4	3.3
Magazine advertisements	2.9	2.6
Billboards	2.4	2.1
Organizational		
The Democratic party	5.3	4.5
The Republican party	3.6	4.1
Membership in religious organizations....	3.4	3.1
Membership in professional or business organizations	3.2	3.4

° The respondents were asked to examine a list of 36 variables that might have some impact on the way they made up their minds about political candidates. They were then asked to rate each of these factors on an 11-point scale (0-10).

Reproduced with the permission of Governor William G. Milliken.

Table II-6 depicts the data in a little different form. All of the factors that may influence the voting decision are rank ordered under three different headings. Each of the three groups is set up on the basis of highest to lowest ratings within the group. This chart represents the perceptions of Michigan gubernatorial voters in May of 1970.

Contacts with candidates, talks with political workers, political brochures, newspaper advertisements, television advertisements, political mailings, radio advertisements, magazine advertisements, billboards, and telephone campaign messages are ten media variables that can be directly controlled or in some way manipulated by the campaign. They can be controlled in the sense that they can be purchased or that the energies of the candidate can be focused on them.

Note that nine of the ten "very important" variables are really not able to be controlled by the campaign. In the "very important" column, the only one that can be controlled is "contacts with candidates." Note also that there are no advertisements in this "very important" group. Think about that, Madison Avenue!

Television news, documentaries, and talk shows are ranked by far as the most important, but notice that newspaper editorials and stories do rank third and fourth. Talks with family is next, followed by radio educational and news programs.

Now, in terms of the ratings of all advertising, brochures ranked 19th in importance; newspapers ads, 22nd; television ads, 24th; mail, 25th; radio ads, 26th; magazine ads, 27th; billboards, 28th; and telephone campaign messages, 29th.

What is most important, then, are those variables which cannot be directly controlled by the candidates. This means that the major campaign communications effort must go through media which cannot be controlled (or purchased) by the candidates.

OK, so what is so new about that? Well, for one thing the analysts and writers who are so hung up on slick political advertising on television—and the evils thereof—are missing the boat when they zero in on television advertising as the major variable in explaining voting behavior in presidential and statewide contests.

Operationally, these findings meant a great deal to our campaign. The strategy for Governor Milliken's campaign was in large part based on them. Let me give you a few examples of how we used these findings in that campaign.

First, we worked from the premise that a campaign must be newsworthy. The candidate must say and do important things for the reporters who cover the campaign and the voters who watch it. In this process, of course, the incumbent has an enormous advantage. If you are handling a campaign for an incumbent and you can't figure out a way to be in the news almost every day, you are either lazy or incompetent, or you happen to be governing Utopia.

Second, when you have some news to release, design it principally for audiovisual coverage. This makes it difficult for reporters *not* to cover it. For example, in television—which is of course the most important news medium—the Governor had his own cameraman who took sound-on film and silent clips of the Governor's campaign almost every day. These 30 or 60-second color clips were sent to 14 television stations throughout the state. Outside of the city of Detroit, we estimated we got better than 60 percent coverage. These clips not only looked like news film but for the most part had significant news content. We used the same technique for radio with the provision of tapes over the telephone.

Another example: We found that major policy statements are best handled through structured press conferences rather than appearances before large audiences in various cities. We also found that in these press conferences we should use audiovisual techniques for the best news coverage. By that I mean slides, films, charts, tables, and so on, with the candidate making the actual presentation.

Now, when you start doing all of these things, you start thinking like a newsman. But, I don't know if that's all bad. The point is you tend to view the campaign as a series of news events. Obviously, when you use these news techniques, it is difficult and hazardous to sell a candidate who is less than genuine. One of the criticisms of the new politics is that it al-

Table II-6. RELATIVE IMPORTANCE OF FACTORS THAT INFLUENCE THE VOTING DECISIONS OF 1970 GUBERNATORIAL UNDECIDED
(May 1970; n = 809)

Very important (5.0 and over)	Important (3.0-4.9)	Not important (1.0-2.9)
Television newscasts	Talks with friends	*Magazine advertisements
Television documentaries and specials	Radio talk shows	Television entertainers
	Magazine editorials	*Billboards
Newspaper editorials	*Talks with political party workers	*Telephone campaign messages
Television editorials		
Television talk shows	Talks with work associates	Movies
Television educational programs	Radio editorials	Stage plays
	*Political brochures	Phonograph records
Talks with family	Talks with neighbors	
Radio educational programs	Magazine stories	
Radio newscasts	*Newspaper advertisements	
The Democratic party	The Republican party	
*Contacts with candidates	*Television advertisements	
Newspaper stories	Books	
	*Political mailings	
	Membership in religious organizations	
	Membership in professional or business organizations	
	*Radio advertisements	

*Factors which can be influenced or controlled by the candidate.

legedly merchandises candidates to an unsuspecting public and newsmen. But if you follow these techniques, you are trying to get the most news exposure for your candidate and not the least.

What about other ways to structure a media campaign based on these findings? First of all, I would build television commercials by using news formats—spots that look like news. Governor Milliken's spots followed a kind of mini-documentary format covering some nine issues of importance to Michigan voters. In one of these 30-second spots we had a little girl holding a dead bird, thereby depicting one of the effects of pollution. The camera then dissolved from the little girl to the Governor who said what he had done about DDT and what he thought might also be done in the future. Then the picture dissolved and a voice-over announcer editorialized by asking the voters to "think about that" on election day. So the commercial was not a hard sell—it depicted the problem, described how it was handled or could be handled, and then asked the viewers to think about it.

I am sure that you are all aware that the day has passed when a candidate can go on television and tell the voters that he is going to solve all their problems. They don't believe it anymore—if they ever did. Any candidate who goes on TV with a hard sell and says he is going to solve all of your problems is destined to lose. If a candidate can demonstrate competence in handling one or two problems, voters will generalize from that to others.

This means, I think, that your television spots are generally going to have to deal with issues. And, by the way, dealing with issues in commercials is news in and of itself.

Another point: you can place your spots in adjacencies next to newscasts, specials, documentaries, and so on. We have also found that undecided voters (ticket-splitters) watch a good many sportscast. You can through the use of news-formulated spots and appropriate adjacencies maximize your exposure to large audiences of ticket-splitters.

Sound-on-film documentaries may be good if they are newsworthy, interesting, and, most of all, believable. I don't believe a 30-minute documentary is very effective in general elections—this may not be true in primaries if you are trying to build a high identity level. I think a 4 or 5-minute documentary might have some utility if it looks like a news documentary.

You should try to schedule the candidate—particularly if he is the challenger—on talk shows. We have found that confrontations on radio and TV are some of the most believable sources of news for voters. People tend to believe a two-person confrontation more than a one-person situation. So if you can get into your message the element of confrontation, you raise the authoritativeness of the commercial.

Newspaper editorials, as Table II-6 shows, are important. We have used them in radio commercials. We put several quotes from favorable newspaper editorials into a 30-second spot in the media markets where the newspapers are located. Radio, as far as I am concerned, has very limited campaign utility. Perhaps its most important function is that of a reinforcing medium.

In order to make all of these techniques effective we need a good communications system with the electorate which feeds the campaign accurate and up-to-date information about the electorate. This can only be supplied by constant polling. I had never been convinced of the efficacy of polling by telephone, but my experiences in the Milliken campaign changed my mind. During September and October, DeVries Associates conducted 5,400 telephone interviews with registered voters. We interviewed four nights a week in 14 different media markets. Based on these polling results we knew the concerns and intended behavior of voters in Flint, Grand Rapids, Detroit, and so on. We could adjust our media strategy to meet those concerns and speak to the relevant issues. In the Michigan campaign, the issue structure changed about the first week of October. It shifted from what Scammon and Wattenberg called the "social issue" to economic problems (*e.g.*, taxes, budget, GM strike, unemployment) during the last three weeks of the campaign. Had we not been polling, we would not have known it; and I suspect that might have affected the outcome of the election.

The point is that the media—outside of the direct control of the candidate—can be used effectively to reach the voters. I consider news and not advertising as the most important variable in a competitive statewide campaign. A study of primary elections, however, might reveal some different patterns.

The last charts are post-election study data taken from a study of undecided voters who committed themselves during the last five to seven days of the campaign. We interviewed on October 27 and 29, then went back and reinterviewed on November 16 to determine the reasons for their movement from indecision to commitment.

For those empirical purists among you, it is with a small amount of embarrassment that I have included these tables from my post-election study. In some cases the number of voters in the data cells is quite small. However, I am interested in pointing out trends to you, and the data of the post-election study corresponded nicely with previous poll findings.

The responses in Table II-7 are grouped by candidate, issue, media, party, and interpersonal orientations. About 40 percent of the people who made up their minds in the last seven days of the campaign could not articulate, or would not, any particular reason for moving from indecision to commitment.

Turn to Table II-8 and notice that the principal reason

given for moving from indecision to Levin—the Democratic candidate—was "issues;" the second most important was "candidate;" third, "party;" and fourth, "media." Now, look at Governor Milliken just below that—the principal reason cited is "candidate;" ten points higher than that cited for Levin. For all gubernatorial undecided who had shifted, the total for candidate-oriented reasons was 25 percent; issues, 18 percent; and party, 9 percent.

In Table II-9, look at the ability to handle the job, and the behavior of the undecided voters who moved to Governor Milliken. This obviously reflects, first of all, the strength of the incumbency, but it also points out the effectiveness of the campaign strategy—to identify Milliken as the Governor and as being able to handle the job.

If you look at the media responses in Table II-10, there really isn't much to generalize about. But I think—based on my other data—that television advertising was not that important is this campaign. Print media in our campaign—at least in the distribution of personalized direct mail and the distribution of 3 million rotogravure sections—were the most effective campaign techniques.

Table II-12 shows the issue structure at the end of the campaign. As I stated earlier, the important issues changed at the end and had become economic. About 56 percent of the responses related to taxes. The education issue in Michigan, too, was really a tax issue. In other words, the bulk of the responses were economic—not "social." There was no social issue to speak of in the last days of the campaign.

In summary, our campaign was decided in the last five days between October 29 and November 3. Second, we used every single possible technique identified with the new poli-

Table II-7. MOST IMPORTANT THINGS IN DECIDING HOW TO VOTE FOR GOVERNOR[1]
(Michigan 1970; n = 206)

Voting decision[2]	Candidate oriented	Issue oriented	Media oriented	Party oriented	Interpersonal oriented	Don't know/ other	Number of respondents
Milliken to Levin	—	—	—	—	—	100.0%	1
Levin-Levin	17.4%	19.6%	2.2%	15.2%	2.2%	43.4	46
Undecided to Levin	16.3	27.9	6.9	16.3	—	32.6	43
All Levin voters	16.7	23.3	4.4	15.6	1.1	38.9	90
Levin to Milliken	20.0	40.0	—	20.0	0.0	20.0	5
Milliken—Milliken	32.5	15.0	10.0	5.0	2.5	35.0	40
Undecided to Milliken	33.8	11.3	5.6	4.2	—	45.1	71
All Milliken voters	32.8	13.8	6.9	5.2	0.9	40.4	116
TOTAL ALL VOTERS	25.7	18.0	5.8	9.7	1.0	40.8	206

[1] The question asked was: "As you think about how you made up your mind to vote for Governor, what are the most important things that helped you to decide?"

All of the responses were grouped into six categories: candidates, issues, media, party, interpersonal, and "other" which included "don't know."

[2] These categories represent behavior shifts (where appropriate) that occurred between October 27 and 29 and November 16.

tics. Third, those registered voters who did not vote would have voted three to one for Sander Levin, and we would have lost. Fourth, those people who did decide in the last five to seven days voted two to one for Governor Milliken—principally, I think, because of our print media (direct mail and rotogravure sections).

In short, as I look against the background of these data, it seems to me quite clear—at least in our state—that candidate, issues, media, and the party are still seen in that order of importance to the ticket-splitter.

The techniques that we used here are not constants. Their effectiveness changes throughout time. As a matter of fact, the effectiveness of campaign techniques can change during the course of a campaign. We've found this with direct mail. At the beginning of the campaign it was totally ineffective in certain areas. Let me quickly describe one experiment. We went into upper-income and middle-income areas that had very high ticket-splitting. One precinct was controlled, and the other was experimental. In the experimental precinct, we sent every registered voter's home a personal letter from

Table II-8. RANK ORDER OF MOST IMPORTANT THINGS IN
DECIDING HOW TO VOTE FOR GOVERNOR
(Michigan, 1970)

Levin voters (n = 90)

Variables	Total	Levin—Levin	Undecided to Levin	Milliken to Levin
Issues	23.3%	19.6%	27.9%	—
Candidates	16.7	17.4	16.3	—
Party	15.6	15.2	16.23	—
Media	4.4	2.2	6.9	—
Interpersonal	1.1	2.2	—	—

Milliken voters (n = 116)

Variables	Total	Milliken—Milliken	Undecided to Milliken	Levin to Milliken
Candidate	32.8%	32.5%	33.8%	40.0%
Issues	13.8	15.0	11.3	20.0
Media	6.9	10.0	5.6	20.0
Party	5.2	5.0	4.2	—
Interpersonal	0.9	2.5	—	—

All gubernatorial voters (n = 206)

Variables	Total
Candidates	25.7%
Issues	18.0
Party	9.7
Media	5.8
Interpersonal	1.0
Don't know/other	39.2

Table II-9. CANDIDATE-ORIENTED RESPONSES BY 1970 VOTING BEHAVIOR
(n = 53)

Candidate-oriented Responses*	Behavior: Levin voters				Behavior: Milliken voters				All voters
	M—L	L—L	U—L	Total	L—M	M—M	U—M	Total	
	%	%	%	%	%	%	%	%	%
Personality	—	25.0	14.3	20.0	100.0	15.4	33.3	28.9	26.4
Ability to handle job	—	—	—	—	—	69.2	58.2	60.5	44.4
Anti-Milliken	—	75.0	57.1	66.7	—	—	—	—	18.9
Anti-Levin	—	—	—	—	—	15.4	4.2	8.0	5.6
Need a change	—	—	28.6	13.3	—	—	—	—	3.8
Don't know	—	—	—	—	—	—	4.2	2.6	1.9

Personality includes: "he tried; he's older; has sense of humor; gets points across well; know him better; he seems best; feel good about him; sounds good; admire him; has 'get up and go'; like his attitude," etc.

Ability to handle job includes: "has experience; better record; is incumbent; has done more; satisfied with what he does," etc.

Anti-Milliken includes: "don't like present system; don't like Milliken's ideas; Milliken isn't very strong; Milliken has us in hot water," etc.

Anti-Levin includes: "don't like Levin; not impressed with him," etc.

Table II-10. MEDIA-ORIENTED RESPONSES BY 1970 VOTING BEHAVIOR
(n = 12)

Media responses°	Behavior: Levin voters				Behavior: Milliken voters				All voters
	M—L	L—L	U—L	Total	L—M	M—M	U—M	Total	
	%	%	%		%	%	%	%	%
Audiovisual	—	100.0	33.3	50.0	—	50.0	25.0	37.5	41.7
Print	—	—	66.7	50.0	—	50.0	50.0	50.0	50.0
Audio	—	—	—	—	—	—	25.0	12.5	8.3

Table II-11. PARTY-ORIENTED RESPONSES BY 1970 VOTING BEHAVIOR
(n = 20)

Party responses	Behavior: Levin voters				Behavior: Milliken voters				All voters
	M—L	L—L	U—L	Total	L—M	M—M	U—M	Total	
	%	%	%	%	%	%	%	%	%
He's a Republican/ Democrat	—	85.7	85.7	85.8	—	100.0	66.7	66.7	80.0
	—	14.3	—	7.1	—	—	—	—	5.0
Vote straight ticket Other	—	—	14.3	7.1	100.0	—	33.3	33.3	15.0

Note: There were not enough responses under Interpersonal media to construct a table.

Table II-12. ISSUE-ORIENTED RESPONSES BY 1970 VOTING BEHAVIOR
(n = 39)

Issue responses°	Behavior: Levin voters				Behavior: Milliken voters				All voters
	M—L	L—L	U—L	Total	L—M	M—M	U—M	Total	
	%	%	%	%	%	%	%	%	%
Parochial	—	11.1	38.4	27.3	50.0	14.3	37.5	29.4	28.2
Taxes	—	55.6	23.1	36.4	—	14.3	25.0	17.6	28.2
Education	—	—	7.7	4.5	—	—	12.5	5.9	5.1
Drugs	—	—	—	—	—	14.3	12.5	11.8	5.1
Pollution	—	—	—	—	—	14.3	—	5.9	2.6
Gun control	—	—	—	—	—	—	12.5	5.9	2.6
State budget	—	11.1	15.4	13.7	50.0	—	—	5.9	10.2
General	—	—	15.4	9.1	—	42.8	—	17.6	12.8
Economic situation	—	11.1	—	4.5	—	—	—	—	2.6
Law and order	—	11.1	—	4.5	—	—	—	—	2.6

° "General" responses included: "good ideas on issues; better approaches to problems; Milliken's program, Levin's program," etc.

the Governor. We asked these voters to respond to the letter by writing or calling the Governor. We didn't get one response; and we didn't shift any of the undecided vote. For that group, all computerized direct mail is considered junk mail. Then we went to a lower-middle-income, blue-collar area which had about a medium incidence of ticket-splitting, and we repeated the experiment. We shifted about 9 percent of the vote from undecided to Milliken. We found out that direct mail, at that point in the campaign, was more effective than television, so we went to a direct mail campaign in selected precincts. My point is that the effectiveness of these techniques not only changes from one election to another, but it is conceivable that they change in effectiveness within the course of the campaign itself.

What Really Happened in 1970

by Richard M. Scammon, *Director*
Elections Research Center
Washington, D.C.

The hard facts of the 1970 elections begin with a brief recapitulation of the Republican and Democrat schools of answers to the question of who won the elections of 1970. If we can get the rhetoric out of the way, we can go on to more realistic evaluations of what the results of 1970 may actually have meant.

Briefly, in the elections to the House of Representatives the Democrats would claim that they gained 9 seats, that this was a referendum on the Nixon Administration, that the Nixon-Agnew blitz was rejected, and that they won. The Republicans would say that to lose 9 seats when they were in control of the White House, measured against the historical losses of much larger numbers of seats in off-year voting, was a great victory, and that they won. In the Senate, with somewhat the same kind of rhetoric, Republicans would say they won 2 seats plus a couple of other ideological tilting seats like those of Mr. Benson in Texas and Mr. Buckley in New York. They would say we won 2 seats, and this was against the trend—a trend which shows that the party in control of the White House should lose seats in the Senate—and therefore we won. The Democrats would say in effect that we lost 2 seats, but were defending 25; and we did so well in 1970 that in '72 and '74, when the numbers of seats up for reelection are relatively equal, we are bound to do just as well or better, and therefore we have won control of the Senate in '70, '72, and '74.

About the governorships the Democrats would say: we won 13, we only lost 2, so we have established ourselves as goody dispensers in a number of state capitals; in the area of reapportionment this will be a considerable advantage to us; and now we can build local state political organizations for '72. And the Republicans would reply: these losses are largely due to local issues, such as taxation, personality, and the like; and goodies aren't as important as they used to be; and besides, if winning these governorships builds up local state machines of great power, how did we happen to lose the 13 in the first place?

Now in all of the schools of answers, there are measures of truth and measures of untruth. In a sense, these evaluations are much like the self-evaluation of a person who applies for a federal job. He fills out his form 57 and he doesn't lie, but he just lets the pristine light of truth shine on different aspects of his career. This is the way it is done in political analysis from either National Committee. They can find in both instances a certain amount of validity to some of their claims, and some of their apologies are not too bad. In a sense, both parties are right.

In a very real sense this was an election of continuity and of stability, though these are not words many apply to American life today. The fact is you had no great swing as you had in '66, which was a readjustment of a psychedelic weekend the Republicans had gone through in '64. Nor did you have action like you had in the election of '58, in which a Republican in the White House was not able to bring in the Congress with him, but suffered grievous losses in the Senate and House election of that year. We just didn't have this kind of movement in 1970.

If you take the vote for Congress all over the country, you'll find that it was a few points higher this year for the Democrats. But there was no great sweep, no great movement of political force. As a matter of fact outside the Middle West the total change in the House was plus one Democratic; and if it is true that the economic bite was a very real one, it is hard to see this reflected in the voting of the great industrial states like Pennsylvania, Michigan, and Illinois, which did not turn in a single change in their congressional representation.

I think that although this election was one of continuity, it was certainly a defeat in terms of the hopes and fears expressed a year ago—the hopes of the Republicans and the fears of the Democrats. At the beginning of the year there was a very serious discussion in Washington of a Republican takeover of the Senate and a very significant Republican gain in the election of the House of Representatives; and against that template, there is no question but that Republicans were disappointed in the results of 1970, and that the Democrats had reason to draw considerable joy from them—but not in terms of any great sweep comparable, say, to '66 or to '58.

Now one may add a final thought: in terms of the general run, besides being an exercise in continuity, this was an exercise in what you might call nonpurgation. Mr. Agnew did not succeed in purging the great mass of "radicals" or "radiclibs" from public life. He did purge a few, but not the great mass. And Mr. Galbraith did not succeed in his effort to purge the majority of the Democratic party from the Democratic party. Mr. Jackson and Mr. McGee are still back in the Senate. And Mr. Galbraith is still back where Mr. Galbraith was.

Now, about the issues of 1970: first of all, foreign policy in Vietnam. I have yet to find any evidence that this was a cutting issue in this election in any save a handful of situations. And by cutting issue I do not mean something people are interested in, I mean something that moves people from a habitual loyalty to something new. Catholicism in 1960 was such a cutting issue it moved both Republicans and Democrats across party lines to new expressions of their political view. Goldwater, himself, was such an issue in 1964. Many Republicans of moderate persuasion left the party to vote for Mr. Johnson, and in the deep South many Democrats left their party to vote for Mr. Goldwater. These were cutting issues, they were issues that moved people. They were not just matters people were interested in, or worried about, or talked about. So it was with foreign policy generally and with Vietnam specifically. These were not issues of major importance in 1970.

Secondly, what about the so-called social issues and the concern of the mass of Americans with the problems of drugs, violence, crime—particularly street crime—student unrest, and the like? The social issues worked in some cases and were certainly significant in the defeat of Gore, Tydings, Yarborough, and Duffey. But I think by the large it's fair to say that most Democratic candidates, against whom this issue was used by the Republicans, were able to neutralize it by their own views; and men like Stevenson and Humphrey were able to convince the electors of their states that they were responsible citizens just as concerned about crime, mugging, and all the rest as the Republicans. By and large, though, the Republicans in their rhetoric shouted with some dismay that the Democrats were running pell-mell to the center (and they may have been right). The result was a Democratic neutralization of the social issue. Most Democrats were able to get off the hook. As a matter of fact, there was even one case in Wisconsin in which the Democrats were able to do television spots showing pictures of the bombed buildings of the University of Wisconsin. Pointing out that the state was under the administration of the Republicans, the TV spot suggested that the social issue of law and order demanded the return of Democrats to public office. This raises an important question about the social issue in '72. When does the social issue start to work against the incumbent?

In terms of the economic issue, it seems to me that while it bit—particularly in some of the upper Midwest farm sections—obviously it didn't bite deeply enough to produce major changes. Certainly it didn't bite as deeply as it had done in 1958. Of course there is one version that holds that Republican candidates in 1970 were really in measurable difficulty in October, and that they were pretty much at the end of the road, and many of them were about to be beaten. Then the cavalry went out and rescued the settlers from the Indians. If true this would indicate (a) the economic issue was biting, and (b) Mr. Nixon was very successful in turning it around. But I must admit I am much less persuaded by that explanation than by the explanation that the economic issue didn't bite very deeply in the first place.

Now if these thoughts about the major issues of Vietnam, the "social" area, and the economic area are valid, then what was the nature of the election, aside from being one of continuity? I think in the largest sense it was a sort of traditionalist kind of election in which there was no basic issue—Catholicism, Goldwater, or Free Silver—which might have had new, broad trends. Democrats gained a bit, though Republicans would claim this was normal and to be expected in an "off-year" vote. Actually personality, organization, money, communications, scandalization—things of this sort—counted a good deal. You'll find the split ticket, which is discussed earlier in this book, and of which many examples can be found in the election in November: the election of a Republican governor in Massachusetts at the same time as those two states elected Republican senators; the opposite in Michigan; the reelection of Reagan, the defeat of Murphy. These are instances in which personality, organization, communication, scandalization, and local issues were made significant by the absence of really cutting, larger issues on a nationwide basis.

What about some of the side effects of this election, some of the side questions? First, was there a TV blitz? You may remember that in the weeks before the election there were articles in the press about the mysterious gnomes of the image-making business. And then after the election we read stories about the three-inch high mysterious gnomes of the TV business.

Second, what about the student blitz discussed so much in May? A colleague of mine who was at the University of Chicago says that "when they went off on their two-week holiday, a hundred to a hundred and fifty students became involved in politics, many studied, and the others went to Miami." I can imagine no area of major activity regarded with more hope and fear than the movement of the students into politics six months ago, and more denigrated—and wrongly denigrated—just before and just after the election.

Third, was there a Nixon-Agnew blitz? There is little evidence that the White House commitment created great movement one way or the other. It reinforced the faithful and turned off the unfaithful, and that's about it.

Lastly, ecology and environment did have some effect in the election. But so often ecology and environment ceased to be a cutting issue because one must have something to cut. And I have yet to find a candidate campaigning for dirty air and dirty water. Usually the ecology issue comes down to a question of local circumstance involving economic development versus potential pollution. This is really the issue in Machiasport, it was the issue in South Carolina, it is the issue involved in building a nuclear plant in Minnesota. Which of these things do you want? Obviously in politics, you're trying to find the most of the good with the least of the bad. But in most instances, except for expressions of general belief in the addition of the ecological world to motherhood, you find little of the impact of the environment in this particular election.

Now if these are the facts of 1970, what does this tell us, if anything, for 1972? The answer is—it doesn't tell us very much. New politics is an odd phrase; it started off being a hallmark of McCarthyism. On election night it was claimed by Mr. Buckley, whom you may have seen on television saying, "I am the new politics." Now it has come to be regarded as essentially a mechanical evaluation of the new ways of reaching people. And I think the last may be more valid than the other two. In that sense you have found or will find here more of the examples of the kind of new professionalism available as the campaign handler begins more and more to replace the party. Not in terms of the loyalty described earlier in this book but in terms of who handles the work, who does the modern equivalent of getting the turkey and the ton of coal to reach each family in the precinct. And as the party strength weakens, this, of course, will become more and more important.

Television
and
Image
Making

Discussions about the use of "the media" in political campaigns usually begin and end with television. So it will be in this section, although print and radio still remain important campaign tools.

Television is the medium without which no big-league politician can do—if he wants to win. And, unless he can dream up some dramatic and cost-free way to capture television's attention, he has to pay a fortune to use it.

Money and the manner in which the image-makers sell candidates have created controversy and problems—the magnitude of which are matched only by the power of television. Television itself has become a political issue.

In this chapter, four men take different looks at the picture.

Lawrence Laurent, TV-radio editor of the *Washington Post*, sets the scene with a brief historical look at the rise of television in politics and the development of controversy.

In the second piece, Frederic Papert, founder of Papert, Koenig, Lois Companies, Inc., assaults the notion that image-makers can work miracles with candidates.

Jay Weitzner, president of Broadcast Placement Co., follows Papert with suggestions for handling candidates on television and a call for extensive research.

The final chapter in this section is by Robert D. Squier, president of the Communications Company. Squier gives his views on the urgent need for campaign spending reform.

Television
Becomes
a
Political
Issue

by Lawrence Laurent
TV-Radio Editor
The Washington Post

The takeoff point for any discussion of "The Media and the New Politics" begins with the realization that television, itself, became a political issue in the 1970 campaign. I, for one, am surprised that it took so long.

To explain my surprise, I recall a panel discussion that took place four years ago at a seminar of the Federal Communications Bar Association in Williamsburg, Virginia. One of the panelists was Carroll Newton of the Batten, Barton, Durstine & Osbourne advertising agency (BBD&O), and he is usually credited with having introduced the political "spot" advertisement into national politics. He told the Communications Bar Association that when the one-minute commercials were made (in behalf of General Dwight D. Eisenhower) in 1952, many of the television stations refused to broadcast such commercials. Their refusal was overcome, he said, only by bringing to bear the entire economic muscle of BBD&O upon the stations.

Apparently, in broadcasting, a four-year span is long enough to create a "long established tradition," for by 1956 all argument over the merits of the brief TV political commercial had disappeared, and the form was being used by both the partisans for President Eisenhower and for Adlai Stevenson.

The 1956 campaign, by the way, brought the first real apocalyptic vision of where the TV political commercial would lead the American electorate. This vision came from a writer named John G. Schneider in his novel, *The Golden Kazoo* (New York: Rinehart & Company, Inc., 1956). He had a kind of monstrous science-fiction nightmare of a candidate who conducted a national television giveaway program to win votes. According to Schneider, television as "The Golden Kazoo" would dominate politics in 1960.

The second major phenomenon (the first being television itself, having become a campaign issue) is the overdue recognition that television is the main factor in escalating campaigning costs. This has led Federal Communications Commissioner Nicholas Johnson to suggest, "You can buy the whole damn country for $58 million."

One further historical note: at almost any annual convention of the American Society of Newspaper Editors (ASNE), you can be almost certain to hear at least three speakers quote from a letter that Thomas Jefferson wrote to his friend, Edward Carrington, on January 16, 1787.

Here's what is usually quoted: "The basis of our government being the opinion of the people, the very first object should be to keep that right; and were it left to me to decide whether we should have a government without newspapers or newspapers without a government, I should not hesitate a moment to prefer the latter."

That is a lovely thought, but I suggest that it is absolutely and totally meaningless unless one quotes the sentence which Mr. Jefferson immediately added: "But I should mean that every man should receive those papers and be capable of reading them." (Paul Leicester Ford, ed., *The Writings of Jefferson*, 10 volumes (New York: G. P. Putnam's Sons, 1892-1899), vol. 4, p. 370.)

And if one doesn't omit the rarely cited qualification, I would suggest that the possibility of attaining Mr. Jefferson's ideal didn't become realistic until the arrival in the 20th century of the new electronic media, capable of bypassing illiteracy and making possible the free flow of information to millions of citizens who would not, could not, or did not receive that information in print.

Good Candidates Make Advertising Experts

by Frederic Papert
President
Papert, Koenig, Lois Companies, Inc.

I wish that this book had been written before 1970 and the unsuccessful Ted Sorensen and Charles Goodell campaigns in which we had a hand. For years we got a lot of mileage out of Jacob Javits', Robert Kennedy's, and George McGovern's victories; we spread the word that we had never been in a losing campaign, which, in fact, we had not; and let the political world attribute to us great political skill, hence power. A far more important truth, however, has always been that good candidates make political advertising experts. It simply is not the other way around.

I can't think of a more useless way to spend time than listening to political pundits whose specialty is advertising. Political advertising does not have a life of its own any more than political polls have a life of their own; and there is nothing more pathetic than the campaign year ritual of politicians

96

and their staffs grubbing through the remnants of former campaigns looking for the pundit to lead them to office. What's sad is that they overlook the real key, which is the candidate himself, whose zeal and commitment are the qualities that make people want to vote for him.

To the extent that advertising can help illuminate those virtues, we can play a role. But the notion that we are able to "create" winners, or even to remove warts, is nonsense. We can only reveal. We can help show the candidate at his best; we can accentuate the positive. And we can even hide the candidate, as was done in Rockefeller's 1966 campaign, when the voters of New York were subjected to millions of dollars worth of commercials in which the Governor was neither seen nor heard. But to an audience not unfamiliar with the techniques of television advertising, even *that* was revealing.

What we cannot do is create. We can't make the voters believe that a dummy is smart, a bent man straight, a follower a leader, a bad man good.

Winners have many advisors; losers do it on their own. Even though (in our defense) Papert, Koenig, Lois disclaimed credit, always arguing that our main talent lay in picking winners in the first place, our clients' victories led other potential clients to our doors. We were smart enough to turn down most of them.

We've tried to be good revealers. We've known enough not to get between the candidate and the voters, not to obfuscate the candidate's virtues with advertising techniques—*our* virtues. And because we believe it, we've always tried to concentrate on the candidate, to let him discuss the issues if there are issues, to talk about what he regards as important. By doing so, we've given the voter a close look at the man, eyeball to eyeball; and on the basis of that the chances of the right man getting elected are improved.

Do we sound wise and professional and even brilliant? The most successful political television commercial we've ever done was for Robert Kennedy in his 1964 New York senatorial race. We arranged a question-answer session with several hundred Columbia University students. We encouraged them to give vent to their antagonism toward Kennedy (they were very antagonistic); and that, in turn, brought out Kennedy's real self, both in his answers and in his final five-minute, nonpartisan pep-talk/lecture. We videotaped it all and put it on the air. One half-hour commercial included questions, answers, and speech; another was the five-minute speech alone. And in the week they were on the air, what appeared to be a losing campaign (Kennedy's opponent had gone ahead in the polls and seemed to have momentum on his side) became a 400,000-vote victory.

We had tried other ways to capture the real Kennedy on tape or film for television: street-corner conversations that had worked so well with Javits were no good for Kennedy— the crowds were mobs, cameras were jostled, no one could hear questions or answers; speeches into the camera at studios were disastrous, as they were with Javits—both men froze when lights went on; contemplative strolls through the garden were an even worse disaster—it takes an actor, other-directed, unreal, hollow, to pull it off (Reagan and Nixon come readily to mind). We were getting nowhere, until Ethel Kennedy suggested the students.

It was her idea. The agency saw to it that the cameras were in place, that the tape was edited to size, that the time buys were made, that the material got to the stations and on the air—and that's about as much as advertising experts can do.

My point is that I don't think there are any miracle workers in political advertising. I don't want to spoil Bob Squier's new business pitch to any potential candidates who may be here (if I were running for office, I would try to hire Bob to help run my campaign; he does what he does very well, indeed); but there are limits to what even Bob Squier can do. And if you work in politics and don't understand that, then you're going to get yourself in trouble.

Neither Squier nor Garth nor Guggenheim nor Papert ever elected anybody to anything, and we probably never will. The candidate gets himself elected. Sometimes we help; most of the time we make very little difference.

Handling the Candidate on Television

by Jay Weitzner
President
Broadcast Placement Company

Acting as do believers in voodoo and witchcraft, critics of television's use in political campaigns have naively attributed all sorts of magical powers to the medium. Television in the hands of an unscrupulous candidate, they say, will bend the minds of the voters and send them glassy-eyed and mumbling his name to the polls. Recently the heads of some major advertising agencies voiced their fears of television commercials in politics. Of course, one is to forget the continual onslaught upon our ears and eyes by these selfsame spokesmen. How much veracity can be attributed to men responsible for dancing cigarette packs and green men suffering from giantism?

We must recognize one simple fact: television is a means of communication, albeit one way, in that I talk to you. It can present a point of view in the most stimulating manner, but it certainly cannot force me or you to do something against our will. Yes, an incompetent with a large war chest can inundate us with his commercials but that doesn't guarantee his election. He may make an overkill for name recognition but name recognition doesn't mean election, as we are all aware.

The television commercial serves only to match a message to basic attitudes already existing in the viewer's mind. It can create an impression either favorable or unfavorable, but it cannot make the voter cast his ballot one way or another. The commercial can only illustrate the personality of the candidate or provide him with a platform to raise issues.

Now to the original premise of this book—strategies in the new politics: strategy implies a course or plan of action. And there are three strategic periods of concentrated exposure for the candidate: predeclaration, declaration, and the campaign.

The predeclaration period gives the candidate the opportunity to present himself to the electorate on a somewhat informal basis. He has the opportunity to appear on a variety of entertainment and nonentertainment programs. The amount of free exposure time that is given to him by stations is not limited by equal time rulings of the FCC. The frequency with which he appears is limited only by the interest in the candidate and the story that he has to tell. It is our belief that during this phase the candidate should grasp any opportunity for exposure that is offered to him or is created by his staff. It is during this period that the candidate can take on a three-dimensional personality. He will be able to establish a more intimate relationship with the electorate by letting them see facets of his personality that will not come across during the actual campaign. He'll be able to satisfy that universal curiosity we all have about what goes on behind the scenes in the lives of our public officials. Depending on the type of program appearance, he will be able to tell a joke, play the piano, or go wherever his interest lies.

The declaration is a nonevent staged for the benefit of the news media. It is a nonevent because up until the big day the candidate has vigorously skirted a positive or negative statement regarding his candidacy, but back in our minds we know he's really going to run. The event is staged in that he will be talking to groups of his own supporters who will loudly cheer his every word. It is one of his big days, and possibly at no other time during the campaign will the news media be as kind to him. He is the star and will be treated as such. The scope of questions will run from, "Why are you a candidate?" "When did you make up your mind to run?" to the inevitable question asked of his wife, "Are you happy that he's running?" But that should end the honeymoon.

From then on, if the news media is doing its job, he will be on the spot every time a camera is focused on him or a microphone is held to his mouth. He will be on the offensive as well as the defensive. He is now a member of that uniquely American species—a candidate on the campaign trail.

Let's take a closer look at a prototype candidate. He should have one or more of those characteristics to which we all aspire—he should be attractive, dynamic, have the look of a winner, be likeable, warm, and human. Basically he should have all those preconceived traits that we expect our leaders to possess.

As a result of continual exposure to television, we have learned to project characteristics of our television heroes to our political heroes. We want them to be articulate and also look competent enough to handle the office they are seeking.

They should exude confidence and assuredness, for it is the man we are looking at and not so much his message that is all important. We tend to like and judge people by their style and appearance. Our memories of words fade long before we forget the physical impression of an individual. We recall in terms of overall impressions.

I am not trying to create the impression that I advocate ignoring what the candidate has to say or even brushing it off, because words and their misuse can and do create negative images in our minds. The pompous verbalizer, the pedantic phrasing of an arm-waving candidate will almost immediately foster rejection in the minds of the electorate. I prefer candidates to use words that create pictures in the mind. Let him speak in short, nonlegalistic phrases. The taxpayer should be spoken about as a person and not as some faceless member of the constituency. Money should be talked about in terms of the individual and not in millions of dollars and the taxpayer in general. As a viewer I identify much more easily with a problem or an issue when it directly refers to someone I can identify with as a member of my own peer group.

One of the greatest problems facing the media specialist is that one candidate who just cannot come across the tube. He may have all the negative characteristics I mentioned before plus some of his own. What do you do in a situation like that? Keep him away from cameras, shoot stills, show only reaction shots? None of these is a solution. Try to enlighten the candidate and he will invariably answer—"Pompous, stiff . . . who me?" The poor guy has been getting it from all quarters. Everyone in his personal or political family at one time or another has given him advice. For one appearance they've told him he was too up-tight, and for the same appearance another guide and mentor will say he was too relaxed. So by the time the media specialist gets to him he has been so overwhelmed with advice that he even rejects the specialist's. It is at this point that the media man must call upon whatever psychological abilities he has in order to help the candidate display his strong qualities and suppress his weaker ones. The candidate will reject the concept of role playing in order to reach the electorate. But he must be convinced diplomatically that what he is doing is not creating a role as would an actor but rather enhancing his abilities to reach the electorate.

Extreme care should be taken with the candidate's physical appearance. For television, a competent make-up person should be on hand. And never let a news photographer within a mile of a candidate being made-up. For the same reasons, don't allow retouching while he is on the studio floor unless it is a closed set. Lights should be checked—hopefully with a stand-in of the same height—for all candidates but especially those wearing glasses or who have deep-set eyes or extremely white hair or bald spots.

The television commercial—and it may sound strange to hear this—is not intended to be seen or heard as a single entity existing just for its own sake. Rather, it is supposed to create an impression in the mind of the viewer by involving him in an event. Commercials do not sell; all they can do is create a favorable environment.

And this environment can only be created through the marriage of attitudinal research and the commercial. Therefore, it is to the advantage of the media specialist to work with attitudinal researchers to find those issues that the voter most readily accepts.

Television has an inherent mobility. It moves. It captures time and makes a record of it. I can repeat for an infinite number of times an event that was recorded for television. A still photograph or a printed word is static, it does not move forward or backward. Furthermore, it takes a much more willful effort to ignore that which stimulates two of our senses than that which strikes only one. In other words, that which I see and hear involves me more than that which I just see. Once I am involved, I become a participant and add something of myself to what I see and hear. I add my own impressions and attitudes. I have become part of a circle of communication. I see a politician and add something of what I believe a politician should be. Gestalt psychology says that if we see an incomplete circle, we tend to complete it. Applying this to political communications, we can say that we try to complete as much as possible a circle of communication between politician and electorate by filling in the circle with attitudes learned about the voter and then letting him complete the figure.

This involvement of viewer and candidate can be accomplished in part by making the viewer part of the commercial through the use of such technical applications as the subjective and mobile camera, shoulder shots, etc., the goal being the impression that the viewer is either taking part in the commercial or that it now has really become an event.

If we sit down and attempt to determine one specific formula that will create an impression in the mind of the electorate, we are only deluding ourselves. There is no one answer. And these multiple answers can only be found in the minds of the electorate. Only through extensive polling and researching can we learn if the voter believes that a political controversy exists or that the controversy is between political personalities. How else are we to learn if and what are the political and issue preconceptions of the voters? What is the voter like, and how can we reach him? Is the voter interested in the candidate as a human interest figure, a public interest figure, or as a political leader? Is our candidate trusted or distrusted? Does the candidate match those characteristics considered desirable by the voters?

It is from this information that we are able to develop themes and techniques that will present the candidate to the electorate. For as someone has said, we have gone from the era of the people seeking an audience with a leader to the leader seeking an audience with the people.

Not only are we dependent on attitudinal study for our themes but also for the very language that we must use in communicating with the voters. We must know what symbols should appear in our commercials that are most understood by those we are trying to reach.

Because of the increased sophistication and perhaps the jaded appetites of the voters we believe that the era of commercials showing the candidate staring at the ocean, river, or lake with his jacket over his shoulder; playing tennis or basketball; or talking to the workers, is over. What has defeated it is the fact that we can now direct commercials to specific audiences through the implementation of class and deep-level attitudinal studies. The class grouping or ethnic commercial offers a great potential in terms of its specific appeal, but it is a delicate thing to handle, as it can appear patronizing or even insulting to the audience if mishandled. The regional commercial provides somewhat more leeway in speaking to a specific audience, but it can also have a negative effect in those regions screening opposing commercials. With today's instant communications one cannot say one thing in one region and then take an opposing stand in another.

By increasing our knowledge of the voter and his attitudes and beliefs, we will best be able to reach him with our messages.

Lowering the Cost of Buying Democracy

by Robert D. Squier

President
The Communications Company

Television has been largely responsible for moving politics from the back room to the living room. Unfortunately, in the process, it has also raised the costs of democracy.

There has been a good deal of controversy surrounding this phenomenon in the past several months, principally in connection with the 1970 campaigns and with the attempt to override the President's veto of a TV spending bill.

One must understand that the cost of broadcast air time is what has caused the need for so much money in the first place; sixty cents of every campaign dollar must now be set aside for television and radio.

Why? The reason is very simple. Television has made it possible, for the first time, for a candidate to have direct and personal communication with every potential voter. That communication, however, is riddled with static. It is long on rhetoric and oversimplification and short on responsibility; but it is real, immediate, and a political fact of life—a fact of life we must deal with.

Two things require our immediate attention. First, we must clean up and improve that communication and, secondly, open it up so that a man or woman doesn't have to be rich to use it.

Television is not only the most effective and expensive of the communication media, it also happens to be the only one that is owned by the people. The people own the airwaves and through their government give broadcasters licenses to use their airwaves.

This public ownership has been recently disparaged and deserves some statement of what should be obvious. If broadcasting were free to operate as newspapers, magazines, and the other media, we would be the recipients of the most awful hodge-podge of electronic confusion imaginable. The electronic spectrum is limited. Only so many channels and frequencies are available. (And hurrah, shout many of the present system's justifiable detractors.) As a result, the people were forced to create a monopoly system to control the number of stations that could be licensed. The problem in this country stems from the simple fact that the broadcasters have grown to believe that their license gives them license.

As the system now operates, candidates must pay a ransom to broadcasting stations to use the peoples' airwaves in order to transact the most important business of the democracy—elections. This is wrong. We, the people, own the medium and ought to be able to borrow it back from the broadcasters whenever it suits our public purpose.

The Campaign Broadcast Reform Act of 1970 was just

vetoed by President Nixon, and the veto was sustained. This act would have gone a long way toward removing many of the inequities that now exist in the process of televised political communication.

The President, I cynically believe, proposed a broader campaign reform act at the last hour as a tactic for defeating the legislation. There is no task more important for all of us here to perform than to hold him to that promise I am sure he does not intend to keep. If we don't, we will be affirming a national elections system where an admission price is permanently fixed to the pursuit of public office. We will, by our silence, endorse Political Pay TV.

No campaign spending reform legislation will be complete without the three basic elements of the bill that was just vetoed. It must include:

1. A reasonable limitation on broadcast spending for candidates.
2. Reduction in rates to make candidates the most favored rather than the least favored of the broadcasters' clients.
3. Suspension of S.315 to permit debates between the two major party presidential candidates.

There are those who propose taxing or fund raising schemes to pay for political broadcasting. These proposals simply do not face the simple fact of the peoples' ownership of the airwaves or the profits now being made on political broadcasting.

Others propose that the time be given outright by broadcasters to political candidates. As pleasant as this would be to contemplate, I don't believe such legislation has a reasonable chance of passage.

Broadcasters lobbied long and hard against the present legislation, and they can be expected to continue to do so even more fiercely if the proposed system is noncommercial. Witness the recent action of our own WTOP-TV in the nation's capital.

This station has operated on a free license for 22 years. In this time frame we have seen war, racial strife, recession, a crisis in our cities—a host of 20th century problems. And yet WTOP saved, for its record-setting editorial statement—one that went for 38 minutes of prime evening time—an editorial against the Broadcast Reform Act of 1970. An editorial so short sighted and self-serving as to be beneath the dignity of its Post-Newsweek parentage.

The fact is that the vetoed legislation was a modest proposal for reform and anything approaching passable legislation must follow its general thrust.

It has been proposed that spot announcements be banned or that commercials be screened in advance by a group of "industry elders" who will pass on their veracity. Both of these proposals are distasteful and are probably unnecessary.

Negative advertising and two-dimensional blitzes were the big losers in the 1970 campaign because the people of this country had the good sense to apply their own standards to what they saw. I would prefer the freest speech we can allow to a system that screened or eliminated any part of the paid or unpaid political communications spectrum. The American people know what they want; and if politicians don't begin to give it to them, they will find some new politicians that will.

Let's have a limitation on the *quantity* of television that can be purchased, disallow stations from making political candidates their least favored clients, and leave the policing of the content of our political messages to the American voter.

I would add one final thought which has always served to keep our heads straight when forced to think about the impact of our work on the political system. It is a quote from Daniel Boorstin's book *The Image*.

"We can fabricate fame, we can at will (though usually at considerable expense) make a man or woman well known; but we cannot make him great. We can make a celebrity, but we can never make a hero. In a now-almost-forgotten sense, all heroes are self-made."

The Science
of Polling
and
Survey
Research

Of the techniques used in the new politics today, scientific polling may be the most universal. Most candidates who seek public office want to know if they can win and what the important issues are. It is the job of the political pollster to answer these and other similar questions prior to election day. Good polling involves understanding and predicting what the aggregate of voters will do on election day.

Polling or survey research has two major political forms. The first is the "public opinion poll," which measures a candidate's recognition, recall, and acceptance by the electorate. The second form, the "issues poll," measures voter opinion about the important issues or problems in the campaign.

The first form is generally released to the press for publication, if it indicates that the candidate is winning or closing the gap between him and his opponent. The second form, the issues poll, is used by the candidate and his staff to plan the approach, direction, and strategy of the campaign.

Political polling, like the computer operation in campaigns, is becoming more sophisticated. Pollsters are not only interested in what the issues or problems are but in what solutions the voter offers for these issues or problems. Pollsters are interested in what television and radio programs the voter likes, as well as his favorite newspaper. Pollsters want to know whether or not the voter splits his ticket and why he does so. In short, the pollster discovers who the voter is, what the voter thinks, why he thinks the way he does, and how he will vote on election day.

It has been said that "politics is an art, not a science." The political pollster, however, is close to proving that the art of politics may be polling at its best.

Our first contributor in this section is Harry W. O'Neill, senior vice president and director of Opinion Research Corporation in Princeton. His company does extensive work for candidates and commercial clients and did the work for the Nixon campaign. He has overall responsibility for the opinion research division, in which he handles every area of research other than marketing.

John d'Arc Lorenz is president of Cyr, Picard and Associates, specializing in attitude and issue research. Mr. Lorenz was most recently involved in campaigns in New York State during the 1970 elections.

Oliver A. Quayle III, well-known national political opinion analyst, is based in Bronxville, New York. He has an international reputation, and in the elections of 1970, he handled about as many candidates across the country as any national pollster.

Tully Plesser is president and chief executive officer of the Cambridge Marketing Group. Before the formation of this group he was vice president in charge of market planning and research for Interpublic Group Companies, which used to be McCann-Erikson. He also has an outstanding national reputation; he has worked for such candidates as Richard Nixon, Edward Gurney, Jacob Javits, Walter Peterson, and John Lindsay (in the 1969 campaign).

Russell D. Hemenway is Director of the National Committee for an Effective Congress. He has been involved in observing polling operations in politics to make certain that they are a legitimate and ethical part of the political process.

Gathering Intelligence through Survey Research

by Harry W. O'Neill
Senior Vice President
Opinion Research Corporation

Those involved in managing political campaigns are placing growing emphasis on the media, are increasingly interested in sophisticated survey research, and are developing a greater appreciation for the potential of the computer—from maintaining voter lists to the simulation of voter behavior. Although "art" will never be removed from campaign management, the "science" of politics is maturing. Accompanying more "scientific" campaigns is an upsurge of interest in and concern about the techniques employed—the ingredients of the new politics of political campaigns.

Election polls and survey research have become an established feature of the American political scene; and as campaigns grow in complexity, research will play a larger and changing role.

There will be quantitave change—simply, more candidates will use research more often. There will be qualitative change—a greater demand for reliability, for more detailed analysis, for new techniques, for speed of reporting. Also, and quite significantly, there will be a change in when research is conducted—political research will become less time-bound and more of an ongoing process for both the candidate in office and his opposition. There are many factors responsible for these changes. Let's look at a few of them.

A fairly recent phenomenon—that has also been labeled the new politics—is the increase in the number of candidates who bypass the traditional established party structure in seeking a party nomination in the primary election. The nontraditional candidate has a special need for research, as his success at the polls rests not on getting out the usual loyal party vote but rather in identifying and energizing those who can be rallied to his cause—many of whom may not have been previous primary voters.

The nontraditional candidate often is more issue oriented than is the organization candidate. It is not unusual for the nontraditional candidate to be in the race because he is at variance with the party's choice on one or more issues that he considers of great importance. Since he typically enters the campaign with a limited base of support, he needs to identify through research who, among the potential primary voters, agrees with his positions, and how best to reach them. He must also determine the extent to which his stand on the issues might encourage his opposition to come to the polls in greater numbers than usual. If the nontraditional candidate wins the primary election, then, in addition to the usual research needs of a general election campaign, he should find out rather quickly to what extent his primary campaign may have alienated the members of his party who supported his opponent and how to win them back.

Also increasing the need for political research is the plethora of possible issues in a campaign. Which ones can be utilized most effectively to a candidate's benefit? Which issues are really important to the voting public and which important primarily to the columnists? On which issues is the opposition making significant headway? What issues should be avoided, if at all possible? On which issues is the voting public well informed; on which are the voters uninformed or confused? To answer these and other issue-related questions, research is essential. It provides an objective, outside point of view—an easily overlooked ingredient in a political campaign. A candidate feels closest to those persons in whom he believes he can place his trust and with whom he feels comfortable. These people too frequently think much like the candidate. Thus, within the immediate campaign group, alternative points of view on a given issue may not be fully explored. Research provides the counterbalance necessary for planning sound campaign strategy—although we can testify from our Goldwater experience that there is no guarantee that unpopular findings will be accepted readily.

Another factor: today there are more and more politically viable minorities who cannot be ignored. While in and of themselves many of these minorities may not account for many votes, they are increasingly active and vocal and receive disproportionate coverage from the media. Thus, they are in a position of potential influence beyond their actual numbers. And so they are becoming the focus of political research. The result is either special studies, often probing attitudes in depth, or supplemented samples so various minorities can be broken down into adequate size for reliable analysis.

The increasing use of media, particularly television, should lead to an increase in research. The media expenditures in a major campaign can be enormous. Thus, the campaign research effort should be aimed at measuring the effectiveness of advertising and other coverage the candidate receives—and that of his opponent. What is the degree of awareness of his media exposure? Who is being reached—those persons who can still be coaxed over to his side or only those people who already support him? What messages are actually being registered? Are they the intended messages? How about the candidate's style and voter reaction to it? The answers to questions such as these are useful not only in the campaign being appraised but also for the planning of future campaigns. Certainly the size of media expenditures justify, if not demand, an evaluative effort.

One factor leading to qualitative changes in political research is that political campaigns today move along at a much faster pace than ever before. An event occurring in one place is known almost instantaneously everywhere else. Research data that take weeks—even days—to gather and process may be outdated by the time they are reported. In a major campaign a candidate may find it most useful to have in place a system geared to follow the continually changing political scene. During the 1968 presidential campaign, Opinion Research Corporation had such a facility operating for the Nixon campaign from mid-September to election day. It was a centralized WATS line facility capable of producing several hundred interviews daily, seven days a week. Certain important issues and aspects of the campaign were constantly tracked; questions could be added or deleted on a moment's notice. Thus, on the night of Humphrey's September 30 Salt Lake City speech, in which he altered his stand on Vietnam, we were able to report the latest voter opinion on many aspects of Vietnam within 3 hours of receiving the request. Also, within 48 hours of President Johnson's announced halt to the bombing of North Vietnam, we could report the reactions of voters nationwide and the effect of Johnson's decision on candidate choice.

Anticipating the effects of certain actions that a candidate or his opponent might take is another important area for political research. Selecting various campaign tactics in advance, the candidate can get an indication of what reactions to expect. For example, a major problem facing the Nixon forces in 1968 was how to deal with the Wallace candidacy. While the Wallace supporters were basically Democrats, a large proportion preferred Nixon over Humphrey in a two-way race. How then to win them over? There were several possible strategies, and the possible voter response to each could be postulated and evaluated based on an anlysis of survey research data. The strategy decided on was to use extreme caution in discussing Wallace himself—no personal attack—and to stress constantly the argument that Wallace could not win. While this strategy, in the final analysis, may not have converted many Wallace supporters, the alternative strategies available probably would not only have been less effective but decidedly negative in their impact.

To be maximally useful, political research needs to dig beneath the surface of a campaign—both in the questioning procedures and in the analysis of the data. Often it is not enough, for instance, simply to know the level of support for a candidate. Unless he is far out front, this information is not of much use. What is needed is a measure of strength of support. ORC has developed a Candidate Commitment Scale based on candidate choice, strength of feeling about that choice, likelihood of change in candidate choice, and party preference. This measure has proved highly predictive of how voters ultimately voted, as ascertained in post-election surveys.

The panel approach to campaign research makes possible the important study of campaign dynamics. The main component of the panel study is an intensive base survey to provide benchmark information against which campaign events and changes in candidate choices can be measured. This is accomplished through a series of follow-up interviews with the same respondents throughout the campaign. The purpose of the follow-up waves is to measure the impact of the campaign as it moves along, to pinpoint changes in voter attitudes, and to relate them back to possible causes. This type of research design is capable of providing very specific information as to why changes are taking place and among which groups, all within narrow limits of statistical error.

As part of the Nixon campaign research, we conducted panels in 14 states simultaneously—each comprised an intensive base survey and three follow-up surveys. The total effort involved some 30,000 interviews.

Lastly, a comment about the need for ongoing survey research: our experience has shown that in many elections the large majority of the voters have pretty well decided on their candidate choice by the start of the formal general election campaign. Thus, the persuasive action of a candidate probably must take place long before election day, long before the actual campaign. For this reason, it is necessary not to limit research to the narrow time constraints of the formal campaign but rather to undertake a program of ongoing research. This is particularly important for the successful candidate who is now in office—proposing legislation, voting on legislation, being reminded of his campaign promises, making the headlines. His reelection campaign, in effect, begins the day he is sworn into office; and it is to his advantage to monitor his performance and to keep in close touch with the opinions of his electorate.

Recently, we participated in a project undertaken at the request of the New York City Budget Bureau, financed by the Fund for the City of New York, and supervised by the Vera Institute of Justice. We conducted surveys in New York City concerned with police services and neighborhood safety, narcotics, education, and health services. Although these were not political surveys—their purpose was to investigate the usefulness of survey research as a source of information for governmental decision making—they demonstrate the value of ongoing research, particularly to the man in office. In releasing the surveys, the sponsors said in part: "Facts were obtained in areas where only impressions had been available previously, and in several cases the survey information ran contrary to the expectations of government planners and other experts . . . survey techniques would be useful in providing policy, program, and background information; and they could be used as a means of detecting issues, soliciting suggestions from the public for solutions to particular problems, and for testing public response to governmental policies and programs."

In closing I want to state my firm conviction that survey

research is communicative, not manipulative. It is one of several intelligence sources, the value of which depends, first, on the quality of the research itself and, second, on the ability of the recipient to utilize it. There is nothing sinister or mysterious about survey research. It is simply planned feedback.

Probing for Political Attitudes

by John d'Arc Lorenz
President
Cyr, Picard and Associates

I am going to begin by listing briefly the uses of survey research in the modern campaign, for a simple reason. A great deal has been said about the "communicative" possibilities of survey data and somewhat less about the manipulative possibilities, but we have not emphasized what it is about these data that makes them so useful. I would like to discuss, then, the special characteristics of the data.

Perhaps the most striking characteristic of good modern data is its unit flexibility. With the use of good demographic data, sensitive sampling techniques, and the computer, we can combine and recombine data in an almost endless series of units of different sizes and kinds.

The most basic of these is the geographic unit, which can be as small as the precinct or as large as the country. The geographic unit, which is also political, lends itself to the pinpointing of issues in an area—where, for example, is jet noise a problem? Where do people complain about rats and substandard housing? Does the presence of these issues in these areas coincide with the information we already have about the areas? If the issue is a general one, such as pollution, where is it mentioned with greater intensity? Where is it not mentioned at all? Are there any physical features which might explain this? By the same token, the geographic unit helps "telescope" issues. If one issue is mentioned frequently in this precinct, how is it distributed over the whole ward, congressional district, etc.? What is its citywide (or statewide, or nationwide) pattern of frequency? Needless to say, this aspect of data use includes invaluable comparisons which can be made with other available units of geographic data— health areas, police precincts, transit service areas, etc.

The geographic breakdown of data is the *raison d'être* of the computer-letter aspect of a campaign. It can also provide essential leads to the scheduling and advance specialists, by giving them an overall picture of the candidate's recognition and popularity over his area. And it is indispensable to the research section and to the candidate in helping them to develop their issue research, to seek effective problem-solving positions, and to emphasize locally relevant issues.

More difficult to prepare, but even more valuable, are the various demographic units—age, sex, socioeconomic level, education, ethnic affiliation, housing type/density, and so forth. It is in terms of these units that most of the vital elements of survey data are compared and correlated—issues, word usage, media usage, information level, and especially attitude patterns. Are most middle-aged, middle-income, white, Anglo-Saxon, college-educated house owners concerned about narcotics? And do they use the term "narcotics" or "drugs" or both? And why? The "whys" that present themselves in the interpretation of demographically broken-down data are endless, and they often serve as a major creative stimulus in planning campaign strategy.

Another characteristic of survey data is its adaptability to the changing requirements of the campaign. Surveys can be used in various forms throughout a campaign: to spot-check recognition, to measure the effect of a press release or local candidate appearance, to keep track of a local issue, to investigate questions raised by earlier "waves" of data collection. In-depth interviews can be conducted to try to unravel a problematic emotional issue that is important in the campaign. Information level checks can be made to see which areas need more literature or a more detailed explanation of an issue.

Finally, survey data is being opened up as a sensitive tool in the examination of political behavior. New types of perception studies help us understand why people react to some issues and candidates the way they do. Closely related to this kind of study is attitudinal research, which explains some of the motivation behind people's long-term attitudes about issues, the political structure of the country, and their own relation to both of these. New forms of semantic analysis shed light on reasoning patterns and common associations, on "loaded" words and on changing shades of meaning related to the media barrage to which Americans are continuously exposed.

From this overview of the characteristics of data and their use, it can be seen that survey data represent the only element of a modern campaign which is uniquely "of the people" and "by the people." The people are the data source, and the successful interpretation of data depends on its arrangement in units which sensitively reflect the existing pattern of ideas of the public. This fact, however, is no guarantee that the information so carefully derived will be used "for the people." Indeed, sensitively gathered and analyzed survey data have an inherent manipulative potential of staggering proportions. Let us take, as an example, a hypothetical situation involving data which indicate the voters' level of education and information on a certain issue, let us say, the welfare issue. Candidate X, an unscrupulous person, knows that Candidate Y has taken a "liberal" position advocating, among other things, increased welfare payments. Candidate X possesses data which tell him that the voters in precinct A tend to be blue-collar workers with a high-school educational level. The data also tell him that these voters do not understand the welfare system, and that they hold an incorrect belief that many welfare recipients are employable males who refuse to work. He further knows that the voters themselves place a high value on "working for a living" and that they resent taxation. Finally, he knows that the media-use pattern and educational level of these voters are likely to prevent them from obtaining accurate information about the facts of the welfare issue, or from being exposed to the logical details of Candidate Y's "liberal" positon. The possibilities for exploiting the emotional reaction of the public and damning Candidate Y on this issue are obvious. In fact, many of us can cite examples of similar opportunities for manipulation which have been fully exploited, even to the designing of scurrilous campaign literature for specific localities.

This is not to say that political manipulation is new—in fact, it has been with us for centuries—only that is is "improved," in the same way an effective people-oriented campaign is improved by good data. Whereas before, manipulative tactics required, ironically, a fairly sensitive first-hand knowledge of one's constituency (the "machines" of the old urban wards are an example), they now require only a good set of data and an eye for the possibilities.

We feel that this danger ought to be thoroughly considered and discussed, not only among professionals in survey research but before the public. Too much energy is frequently devoted, by public critics and the press, to poking fun and accusations at the voting-behavior or "straw" poll and its numerous misuses. It is questionable whether this type of poll ever had any effect on the public, and by now many people regard it with a very jaundiced eye. Attitude researchers hope that it will soon be superseded in importance by the issue-related types of survey.

Perhaps the most disturbing aspect of the manipulative use of survey data is its sharp contrast to the original purpose and development of survey research. Thomas Jefferson, during the debate which formed the philosophical basis of American democracy, pointed out that public opinion and the free press were the source of the triple powers of government. If this democratic ideal is to be realized, it would seem to find the most appropriate vehicle in the enlightened use of the survey. In addition, we feel that the campaign which uses surveys to probe the public mind and will, and to interact productively with the public, will lead its successful candidate into office with the same kinds of public-oriented motives and techniques he campaigned with. Just as the candidate who runs his campaign on large money contributions may "belong" to his wealthy benefactors when he takes office, so the candidate who runs on public issues and public approval belongs to the people, and may remember his debt.

Charting the Volatile and Shifting Electorate

by Oliver A. Quayle III
President
Oliver Quayle and Company

First, let me make it clear that I poll mainly Democrats (but not exclusively), and I want to make it abundantly clear that I did not poll for Mr. Gore. I did poll for Mr. Hooker, the Democratic candidate for Governor who lost—but not for Mr. Gore.

To me the most phenomenal finding of the 1970 elections and of recent elections was that while people seemed settled where they were in 1970, during the *process* of settling, they moved around more than we have ever before observed. Anybody involved in a modern political campaign who takes it for granted that things are settled in August or September is simply kidding himself. That desperate struggle for a winning share of the votes now goes right down to the wire.

In Minnesota (in April 1970, I think) we asked a basic question on Vietnam to potential voters: whether they were hawks, "Nixon's," or doves. We had occasion three months later to do a telephone panel study, which means going back to the same people. We found that 41 percent of all the voters in Minnesota had changed their position on U.S. policy in Vietnam between April and June, and I don't just mean moving from hawk to Nixon. During this period some doves became extreme hawks, some moved to support Vietnamization, and some hawks became doves. The movement was of every kind. There was an enormous switch, so much so that we almost didn't believe our data. Then we did the same study in Connecticut and found the same amount of movement. Other panels in states all across the nation showed equal amounts of movement. Our average change on Vietnam was 40 percent.

This might be partly an artifact of Vietnam and the general U.S. confusion of American voters as to what our policy should be there, but we were so intrigued with this that we began to look at our data in terms of people telling us how they were going to vote. In other words, we did panels to observe change in voting intention. In the same length of period—three months—in the gubernatorial and senatorial elections in New York, we found a 41 percent shift. This doesn't mean a 41 percent shift in the overall standings, but 41 percent of the people moved from one candidate to another, or moved from one candidate to undecided, or from undecided to a candidate.

So I am convinced that American voters at this time are flopping all over the place. Voter opinion is extremely volatile, and the modern campaign manager who slows down his effort in the home stretch because he is "home free" is asking for trouble. With this kind of movement taking place, the name of the game is to go all out in order to minimize trends away from a candidate and maximize trends toward him.

I think that is the biggest lesson we learned in the 1970 election.

Eliminating Guesswork through Research

by Tully Plesser
President
Cambridge Opinion Studies, Inc.

The division at Cambridge that engages in wide-range political research is called Cambridge Opinion Studies. In 1970 we were active in 11 states. We do accept assignments only from Republican candidates.

We have always objected to the terms "pollster" and "polling," because they connote a kind of activity that is limited to going out and asking people a question and then reporting what the people said. I don't think that that's the function that we have been serving in campaign organizations, and I don't think that it's the function that is most valuable in winning elections.

I would submit as an alternative term, one more appropriate for our firm's activity and maybe for the entire field, the words "communication research." We have seen that the primary value of voter attitude surveys and survey research is their usefulness in the planning and development of all types of campaign communication. If we accept the term "communication research" to describe our activity in political campaigns, we obviate the need for "guessing" what kinds of studies are required. If you think in terms of communication research, all you have to do is sit down and ask, "What do I need in order to effectively plan my communication?" The various answers to that question will spell out for you what studies you will have to have.

A campaign is essentially a conversation between a candidate and an electorate. If you want to know what to talk about—if that's what your communication program requires—then you have to have studies that tell you which subjects are relevant and interesting and possibly useful as "leverage subjects." Mr. Scammon's phrase, "subjects that will move people or change their opinion," is a good definition. If what you must know in order to have this conversation is what language to use, then survey research can give you the "language" of the issues. We've all learned by now that "conservative" doesn't mean the same thing to everybody, and "liberal" and "law and order" and "crime" do not mean the same things to all people in all situations, so we must learn the language from the survey research.

If in order to have good communication you have to divide or segment the electorate into groups that can be reached by different vehicles or different media, then you have to have segmentation studies in your campaign research. There is no such thing as a total electorate for purposes of communication. The only time the electorate is a unit is when you are counting up who won or who lost. But in planning a conversation, you must think in terms of the different segments of your electorate, and you may have to vary what you talk about and how you talk according to what segment you are dealing with. Campaign research has to make that possible as well.

In order to make a point in a good conversation, you have to find out the vulnerability of your opponent. He may have a weak spot in his emotional makeup, for example. Or he may have an informational weak spot; there may be some issues he does not know enough about, and when you talk about those issues, he's yours. He may have some kind of a momentum weak spot, in the sense that once you get him going in a particular direction, he tends to keep going. That's the art (if there is an art) of conversation.

Through communication research you can also find out the vulnerability of the electorate; that is, where they are vulnerable to your communication. Then your campaign research on issues is made more effective as well.

In a nutshell, we have directed our efforts over the last couple of years, and will direct them in the future, away from overly simplistic measurements of how many voters intend to vote for which candidate. In direct contrast to the work Walter DeVries has described, we are trying to get away from asking people, "What do you think influenced you to vote?" We are increasingly involved in devising more sophisticated measurements of segmentation in the electorate and in exploring better ways of communicating with different segments. How best to communicate with them depends on what terms and issues, what language and what vulnerabilities there are to work with in the course of the campaign conversation. This is what we see as the focus of our campaign research at present and in the future.

Reforming the Political Money Game

by Russell D. Hemenway
Director
National Committee for an Effective Congress

A couple of years ago I was asked what the new politics was, and I said it was old politics practiced by new people. I've since amended my definition of new politics—I think it's closer to Joe Napolitan's. It's how you communicate with people. It's going *directly* to the people instead of going through the party leaders and party organization. Communication, or *how* to get to them, is obviously the new politics. I think James Buckley is wrong in saying that he is the new politics, but since he won you have to consider whether or not he may be right.

Will Rogers once said that the U.S. Congress was the best that money could buy. If he were alive today, I'm sure that he would amend his remarks, because considering the amount of money spent on politics in 1970, we deserve something better than what we've got.

I was very much involved in drafting and managing a reform bill to take money out of politics, the first such bill in the 45 years since the Corrupt Practices Act was passed in 1925. The bill passed the Senate and the House handsomely, was vetoed by the President, and then, just recently, was very narrowly overridden by the Senate. My organization, the National Committee for an Effective Congress, did succeed in creating a climate which we think is going to dictate change and affect the role of money in politics. We do not think we're overstating the case or being overdramatic when we say that the entire system is being threatened and may be subverted by money. You have to be rich to run today, or else you become seriously encumbered by your commitments to those people who put up the enormous amount of money it takes to run for public office.

The danger, of course, lies at the "entry point" to politics—Congress—and not at the presidential level. Some of this money goes to pollsters today, but not very much. Over 50 percent of the money spent in political campaigns in 1970—at least 50 percent in every senatorial race—was spent on broadcasting. This is obviously, as Mr. Nixon said, one of the holes in the sieve, but it's the largest hole in the sieve, and it must be plugged.

The amount of money spent on trying to ascertain what the people are thinking, how to organize a campaign, where to use your resources, how to develop a theme, and what the issues are—the job of pollsters—is proportionately small. I don't have a figure, but if a hundred million dollars was spent on congressional elections in 1970, I would guess that no more than two to three million went into public opinion surveys.

138

If a candidate says to me, as some did in 1970, "I have no faith in polls, I'm not interested in them, I know more about my state and my constituency, I've won three times," I say, "Go find yourself another source of money; we're not interested in financing your campaign. You're going to lose." It's as simple as that.

Albert Gore had this approach. He didn't decide to poll until very late, and he did very bad polling. He didn't know very much about his state because, in my opinion, his polls were not very well analyzed. I could mention other candidates, but I choose to mention him because he lost, and it's better to mention losers than winners.

In 1956, I heard Adlai Stevenson make a very impassioned and beautiful speech, after which an overzealous reporter jumped up in the back of the room and said, "Governor Stevenson, if every right-minded person in the country votes for you, you'll be President of the United States." And Stevenson's remark was, "I'm sorry. That's not enough. I need a majority."

What we need to find out is how to get a majority. Polling is one way.

The Application of Data Processing and Computers to Politics

Those who have spent tedious hours cutting up phone or voter lists, or copying names and addresses on 3 by 5 cards or envelopes can fully appreciate the impact of a computer on a campaign. So can those faced with the need to select and concentrate limited resources of time, people, and money on those households that are most likely to be favorably affected by campaign efforts.

The ability of the computer to store, sort, and selectively print information releases volunteers from clerical work and permits them to have more actual contact with the voter. The applications resulting from this ability are seemingly endless and increasing with each election. Selective mailing of literature and invitations recruit support; personal letters and "grams" raise money, encourage registration, and get out the vote with proven success. Walking lists and phone canvass lists are becoming standard equipment of the precinct chairman, and precinct vote analysis for selection of target precincts is being used by more managers to concentrate their resources.

It is noteworthy that virtually all our contributors in this section discuss the sophisticated use of this clerical ability of the computer in recent elections and refer to future elections when talking about its controlling and decision-making capabilities. Scheduling of the candidate, allocation of funds, critical path control and simulation are still more talked about than practiced.

Throughout the discussion it is apparent that computer use in politics, though still in its infancy, has made it possible to create political organization overnight and thus poses a serious challenge to those party organizations that do not use these techniques. Television surely creates the image for the candidate, while the computer creates the organization that capitalizes on that image. Personalized contact (print, phone, or door-to-door), made possible or more effective by the computer, requires personal action or involvement that is the key to commitment. The development of optical scanning of mail surveys and phone-canvass results makes two-way communication on a large scale practical. Such a capability is sure to have significant impact on today's politics that are so dominated by one-way mass media.

In this section, five recognized leaders in their respective uses of computers in politics share their experience and techniques.

Frederick P. Currier was assistant research director for the *Detroit Free Press*. In 1962 he became vice president of Market Opinion Research of Detroit and since 1968 has been president of that organization. He has developed political definitions for political strategy, the ticket-splitter approach to behavioral politics—which has involved voting analysis, polling analysis, and other aspects of political management.

Dr. Jack Moshman was in charge of election-night coverage for NBC in 1960 and 1962, and ABC in 1964, 1966, and 1970. He is a fellow of the American Statistical Association, former vice president of the Association for computing Machinery, and a member of the National Research Council. He is currently president of Moshman Associates.

William A. Butcher is president of American Computer Resources of Los Angeles. His firm has developed one of the few reapportionment computer programs that has been successfully used. He was formerly on the staff of Congressman Richard Hanna of California.

Matt Reese began his national political career as executive director of West Virginia for Kennedy in 1960. He was director of operations for the Democratic National Committee from 1961 to 1965 and was national director of the Democratic Party Voter Registration Campaign in 1964. He is president of Matt Reese Associates, a Washington-based firm of campaign consultants.

Richard A. Viguerie has been described as "an enterprising young fellow who will for a fee solicit funds for right-thinking candidates from a mailing list of 500,000 conservatives who in the past have contributed to the campaigns of such as Senator Barry Goldwater, Senator Strom Thurmond, and Senator John Tower." He is president of Richard A. Viguerie Company, Inc., a firm that in 1968 and 1969 mailed over 10 million letters and in 1970 mailed over 20 million letters for political campaign fund raising.

Retrieving Political Information Instantly

by Frederick P. Currier

President

Market Opinion Research Company

The new politics is perceived as a voting system or strategic problem by some, and a manipulation problem by others. I am going to treat it in the first sense of the word and discuss briefly the basic uses that we have seen for data processing and computers—particularly during the 1960's—and where I believe the trends will take us in the future.

The seven basic areas where data processing and computers are used in politics are: voting analysis, voter identification, simulation models, polling, media models, reapportionment, and instant information terminals.

Voting Analysis

Voting analysis developed dramatically, starting in 1960 to 1962, with the ticket-splitting concept which is referred to in detail in the Republican National Committee publications and such books as James Perry's *The New Politics.*[1] This method of analysis not only allowed candidates to make the most of their campaign time in terms of past election behavior but also in terms of alternative strategies with the three key groups: core Democrats, core Republicans, and particularly ticket-splitters.

The ticket-splitter, or swing voter, concept lends itself to extensive statistical manipulation, and the number of ticket-splitter concepts is almost infinite. The main idea behind the concept is that the voter who divides his ballot by voting for candidates of different parties is more open to appeals, ideas, personality, or issue presentations than the straight ticket, or core party, voter is. The concept is particularly useful, of course, in statewide races other than the presidential race where appeals on a particular issue or a candidate's position may differentially affect subsets of the voting audience.

Our company, Market Opinion Research, has worked in more than 20 states in major races in recent years, predominantly in Midwestern and Eastern states. For large states we find it necessary to collect data on voting behavior at the precinct level, clean it, and put it in some sort of data bank. In the middle sixties the analysis became very complex. One could determine which precincts had heavy ticket-splitting by looking at total vote differences between offices going from the highest race to the lowest race, or the reverse. For example, if the total Republican (or Democrat) vote for U.S. senator in a precinct was very different from the total Republican vote for governor, the precinct was heavy in ticket-splitting. Or if the vote for U.S. senator by party was very different from that for a statewide office or a county office, it was heavy in ticket-splitting. This resulted in very complex types of analysis by level and through time comparing results say for 1960, 1964, 1966, and 1968.

The trend now is to go back to a very simplistic form of ticket-splitting analysis. I think the future trend will be some index of ticket-splitting attached to the enumeration districts or the precinct clusters according to grade levels of the race in senatorial, gubernatorial, presidential, county, and statewide elections. In other words, I think we'll simplify this measure once we go through the reapportionment process this year.

Voter Identification and Personalized Motivation

To the extent that ticket-splitters are in fact the key to winning races, which many feel they are, the drive to personally identify them and personally appeal to them with all forms of directed and mass media will intensify in the seventies and beyond.

Voter identification drives to stimulate to greater turnout for key voter groups have used the computer. This trend—an increasing one since 1960—involves building up a data base in which voters are identified by name, address, special interests such as occupation, age, etc., in a form which can be used by the computer. In some states such voter identification covers a fairly large portion of the electorate. The computer can then generate lists for direct mail efforts, computer-printed personalized letters, lists for telephone calling in the last two weeks, and election activities in particular geographic areas. For example, letters concerning a candidate's stand on Medicare can be directed personally to voters over 65; or a letter concerning his views on state or federal support of education can be directed to local members of the National Education Association, faculties of local schools, community colleges, and universities.

Additionally, campaigns can be directed into areas where ticket-splitting voting has been heavy in the past. This is particularly useful for candidates running in closely contested races. In the future these data bases will continue to be enlarged, and direct mail efforts will continue to expand.

Simulation Models

Simulation models in politics moved very rapidly in the early sixties because of the work of Ithiel de Sola Pool.[2] Since then they have diminished.

Simulation models should be divided into strategic simulations and national simulations. I think these models are basically better fitted to statewide analysis for the simple reason that a national election is really an election based on seinging key states. It's not an election in which data based on national inputs is needed on an extremely frequent and accurate basis.

Simulation requires building a massive data bank on a number of variables. Critical to a successfuful simulation is determining the relationships which link the variables. The other key factor is the attitude researchers. They say that they want to measure variables, such as attitude shifts, on a panel basis. Recontacting the same people implies really massive inputs in terms of money. I think what is going to happen to simulation is that there will be panel efforts only in large swing states.

Right now it appears that a series of studies with comparable samples tied together through time is more useful than a massive simulation of the same data.

Polling

Polling has probably increased faster than other market research, and will continue to increase but at a slower rate. The limiting factor in the future will be the length of the interview and the number of variables. In an election study a few years ago, Market Opinion Research measured 110 variables and only accounted for 40 percent of the variance. We always have that problem when designing a system.

In terms of polling and the computer, the annual rate of growth in market research has been about 17 percent in recent years, and in polling in an election year it's probably about 25 percent. I think it's going to be decreasing, though, because one can't really poll much below a congressional level race without taking too large a share of the candidate's budget. In other words, the sample size problem alone inhibits polling at a lower level.

In terms of sampling problems the computer is a tremendous tool. When I was writing the final *Detroit News* polls in 1970, I was looking at nine or ten waves of previous data. I had two different subsamples within the sample, and I took into account both samples before I started analyzing voter behavior. By reevaluating probable voter turnout by areas, I cut down the probable error for an average turnout on the night before the election to within a point (.3) of the final result (which disturbed a lot of people.) I couldn't have done this if I didn't have the computer on the premises.

Media Models

Media models, which include reach and frequency concepts between measured and nonmeasured media such as telephone calls, direct mail, and computer letters, will probably increase in complexity and design. They may be a better answer than political simulation, since the deciding factors are really media determinations as much as strategy determinations.

Those who are concerned with media models know that reach and frequency data really measure media in a very interesting way. Essentially "reach" says that if you hit 55 percent of the adults with a certain medium, and if you go into that medium five times, you may push that reach or total exposures up to around 88 percent because of the probability of hitting additional adults through time. These models in the media field are very complex because they overlap all the media and all the overlaps within each medium. Media models are getting more advanced, although you don't hear as much about them. I think the use of media models will increase.

Reapportionment

Computers are used for reapportionment to merge voting data and population data to reapportion state legislatures, congressional districts, and other political units. It is clear that here the only real limit is the creativeness of the programmers and the capacity of the computers, neither of which seem to be limiting factors.

Reapportionment means essentially getting that MED (Master Enumeration District) tape on the first count of the U.S. Census and merging it against precinct data. In 1971 it turned out to be one messy job and very expensive in some states, but the return on investment is very good. Every state is different, though, in terms of timing and political strategy. These massive data banks will be used in the future to further refine state and congressional electional strategies.

Instant Information Terminals

Terminals have increased dramatically during the last few years when small amounts of information could be transported. If the computer utiolity system continues to expand, it is conceivable that increased data banks will allow the marketing battle strategy to originate from a central point. Or to paraphrase Kahn of the Hudson Institute, it will be a case of our computer against their computer.

One of the problems one has when trying to update a computer is deciding which terminal company or computer utility to choose. It is an economic problem: Which one is going to be in business in a few years? There are only two or three companies that are making money in computer utilities. Given the fact that the phone lines linking the terminals to the mother hen computers have same problems, I think the microwave system is an essential breakthrough. I can see in the 1972 elections a hook-up whereby there could be instant information between large key states. Whether instant information means better decisions is an open question, it seems to me.

There are other hurdles to overcome with terminals, such as the problem of capacity usually needed for statistical problems or apportionment work. The problem of making information strategically available is essentially one of polling data.

I'm not that sure where the system is going to take us. I think we will gave a total system just like that found in the business world.

Dangers and Basic Criticisms

The three principal dangers of voter information are that data processing will be skewered on the same basic ethical question that the national data bank was; that there would be overexpectation of the effect of the use of mass data in a national form; and that total information flows may get so huge that voters will insist on less information rather than letting the total system operate freely.

Some political consultants and pollsters such as Robert Teeter argue very strongly that computers in politics are becoming less useful in terms of key decisions during the precampaign and the actual campaign period. This argument basically says that the critical decisions are stands on issues, voter perceptions of the candidate, and media communication effects. The argument that a computer can massage a large base of diverse political material does not imply to these critics that the computer is becoming more powerful.

The role that the computer will play in the future is the same one it plays today: if it is seen as a huge accounting machine, it will play a housekeeping role; but to the extent users see it as a basis for creative alternatives, it will be a major help in a free and expanding society. Larger and larger data bases imply better decisions.

[1] James M. Perry, *The New Politics, The Expanding Technology of Political Manipulation* (New York: Potter, 1968).

[2] Ithiel de Sola Pool, Robert Albeson, and Samuel Popkin, *Candidates, Issues and Strategies: A Computer Simulation of the 1960 and 1964 Presidential Elections* (Cambridge, Mass: The M.I.T. Press, 1964).

Monitoring the Campaign with Computers

by Jack Moshman
President
Moshman Associates, Inc.

Several weeks ago I was in Houston attending the Fall Joint Computer Conference. The luncheon speaker was Art Buchwald, who remarked that he had been watching the expansion of the computer field and the mushrooming population growth of installed computers. A study that he had made indicated to him that on January 13, 1976, the country would run out of data. He proposed that the government reduce the investments now being made in research projects—military and otherwise—and that data manufacturing factories be established.

Some of the techniques which are well established in management are only now beginning to be applied to political science. I will avoid discussing computer letters, the use of computers for campaign fund raising, and some of the other uses which are more akin to some of the earlier applications by which computers first found their way into American business.

Nowadays, computers are being used more and more to aid in some of those hardline decisions which are the ones that I think are beginning to take hold. I tried to get involved in something of this nature with Cliff White and Joe Napolitan two years ago. We were ahead of our time, I believe. 1972 may be the year, but we may still be ahead of our time. These are what I have in mind.

One of the big problems is to maintain control and continuously monitor a very involved campaign. For example, one minor segment of the total effort is that part of the campaign devoted to television spots. This involves blocking air time, fixing a theme, writing and editing a script, recruiting the actors, producing the show, going back and redoing it because it isn't good, and getting newspaper advertisements written to induce people to watch the show, particularly if it's more than a spot such as a 15-minute or 30-minute broadcast.

All of these tasks must dovetail together in order to be effective. When you combine this very simple-minded example with all the million and one things that are involved in a campaign, from getting the initial people together, recruiting the professional group, recruiting the volunteer group, ordering the various print materials that are needed, and sequencing the events throughout the campaign period, it becomes a major problem. If any activity is delayed or deteriorates because someone's not watching it, certain aspects of the campaign will be affected while others will not.

This type of task, the monitoring of a complex, interacting system, is one of the applications for which I think computers will be used more and more. It enables the candidate and the campaign manager to be able to keep on top of what is going on. The systems as used, and their counterparts in business and in government, enable one to spot where things have fallen behind, what the problems are, and where possibly additional resources can be drawn from one place and put into another so that everything is back on schedule.

Another problem, difficult because judgments must be made, is that of allocating the limited resources available to you among the many competing demands. It involves allocating dollars and people. Dollars can be assigned among many different things. Within a segment you may be concerned about the division between air time and print space. You may be concerned about the division between letters and personal appearances. You may be concerned about introducing individuals from outside a constituency, thus producing an effect upon the rest of the campaign. You are concerned also with the fact that an action favorable to one segment of the constituency may be unfavorable to another. These factors interact with each other. You have to balance them; a computer can be helpful.

A particular concern which is related to the problem of allocation of resources is the very nitty gritty problem of budgeting the candidate's time. A contributor wrote earlier in this book of the situation in New York. The candidate cannot be out of the city more than three or three and one-half days, or he loses the coverage by the New York City stations. How do you balance requirements like these, which are real and are ones that you have to know about, with trying to get the most mileage out of the trip, maximum broadcast exposure, and selecting and hitting the right issue? How do you ensure a proper division among the various geographic locations within a state, and the various types of special interest groups before whom appearances are mandatory at some point? How do you schedule appearances in time? How do you sequence them? And if you just don't have enough time, and you rarely do, which ones should give in favor of others? Judgmental factors are paramount. But they can be built into a computer program that will show you their implications. You may not agree with the computer output, so you throw it away and do something else. The computer program, however, does let you see and evaluate what it is you are giving up, in favor of another alternative.

The foregoing are indicative of applications and techniques which I think have electoral application. There is another body of methodology that I think is particularly important and somewhat special this year. That is the area of legislative redistricting in which one must be concerned with various types of forecasting. The orientation is quite different from being concerned with projecting the results of a particular campaign or estimating which are the major issues. Districts change. There are secular trends over time. There are known changes that will take place because of planned redevelopment areas. There are certain movements into and changes within the suburbs. A redistricting pattern planned in the light of 1968 or 1970 data may be reasonably good in 1972, but inimical to the interests of one party or the other from 1974 on through the rest of this decade. So redistricting plans have to be looked at in the light of movements and trends as well as in the light of existing static history. Strategic planning may dictate that it may be useful overall to give up a position in a particular year, if you are successful the other four election years of the decade.

Of course, the computer can be used for redistricting. It is another illustration of the type of allocation that is made by combining precincts into districts. It's a problem that has been faced in other contexts, such as in combining prospects into territories for salesmen or houses into school districts. In legislative redistricting, an overlay of political savvy and knowledge is of utmost importance. A combination of political and analytical capability provides a range of possibilities that can then be looked at with their alternatives, considering short and long-term implications. It enables the bargaining that takes place to be supported by a store of background knowledge of the implications of any types of negotiated trade.

How Computers Can Help in Reapportionment

by William A. Butcher
President
American Computer Resources, Inc.

There are four general areas in which computers will be used. One area is decision-making, other than decision-making in reapportionment. That's just not our particular bag. We use computers in the other three, and I'll comment on all of them briefly.

First, personal communication. The computer makes it possible now to communicate personally with people in a way that has not been possible for approximately fifty years, when constituencies were extremely small. As constituencies grew larger and larger, it became impossible to communicate personally with voters. Then the computer brought us the computer letter, computer telegram, and other forms of "personal" communication. A computer letter, of course, is nothing new to most people here, but intelligent use of the computer letter has been pretty much neglected. A lot of people used it, but not very many people used it wisely. When used correctly, the computer communication has had an incredible impact, absolutely phenomenal. We have one client who uses computer letters very intelligently and devotes a major portion of his campaign budget to them. Among the 23 campaigns he has handled in highly contested situations he has 23 victories—each ranging from underdog to an even match at the start of the campaign. I don't claim everyone using computer letters wins, because 95 percent of the time the users are not maximizing the great potential.

Another area in which the computer is used is in making your workers effective. My former boss, Congressman Dick Hanna, often described workers in politics as people who use sledge hammers to kill flies, and normally that's just about the accepted level of efficiency for volunteer workers. Computers can be used to transform volunteers into effective workers. Tools such as walking lists can create effective get-out-the-vote efforts, highly productive precinct walking and registration work. There will be more and more sophisticated use of computers in this area in each election campaign.

For the time being, however, let me caution against being too cute. Remember with a computer, if you put garbage in, you get garbage out. I saw one instance in a campaign where the plan was to develop a lot of workers in precincts on a block basis. Voters were telephoned and asked to canvass their street. Each one who agreed was sent a list of the people who lived on his block. Each recruit was told to go to the people on the list and rate each one in terms of his likelihood to vote for the candidate, on a scale from one to seven. When the ratings were returned, the campaign workers would go through the list and do different things for each category. People who hated the candidate were dropped; voters who loved him were forgotten about, except for get-out-to-vote reminders; people in between they'd handle with issue oriented letters, etc. All this was marvelous, and I'm sure it's the wave of the future. But the problem was the garbage they put in. Volunteers who were doing this work at the street-block level were not capable of rating people from one to seven in terms of their likelihood to vote for the candidate. They just weren't. The computer did its job perfectly. It produced a list of voters by block, it gave workers a place to rate the voters, it fed the data collected back into the computer, produced a list of people rated from one to seven, and handled all those people in all the specified ways.

One of the products of this effort was a list of the Democrats who opposed this incumbent Democratic congressman. These names were to be pulled off the lists for election day get-out-the-vote work. Fortunately the list was immense, and sensing a goof up, the campaign workers polled the Democrats on this list by telephone. Almost 75 percent said they intended to vote for their Democratic congressman! I suspect the remainder of the data was about equally as accurate.

The final area, and I believe the one which has the greatest potential impact, is reapportionment. A million dollars spent now will save parties who control legislatures about a billion dollars in campaign funds over the next ten years. Probably the wisest investment any party or any group in a position to control a reapportionment could make is an investment now in computerizing their reapportionment. I believe ten years ago most parties were wrong. They based their district lines on what happened in 1958 and 1960 elections. By 1970 many of those legislative and congressional districts voting patterns had changed dramatically, partially because of the issues and largely because of the tremendous movement of voters which could have been projected in 1960. Even better projections are possible now, and elections will be strongly affected in those states where the reapportioners make intelligent use of the decision-making tools in their possession or potentially in their possession. No matter how effectively you campaign, if the job is done right in reapportionment, it is going to be extremely difficult to unseat the parties who have designed these districts.

Locating the "Switch-Split" Vote

by Matthew Reese
President
Matt Reese Associates, Inc.

An old-time, practical politician taught me the mule theory; if you hit a mule in the head every morning at eight o'clock, he learns to do either one of two things; he learns either to enjoy it or to duck. We've learned to use computers because we had to use computers, not because we knew anything about them in the beginning. We use them in a rather sophisticated way. We don't know everything to do in a political campaign, but in general we know what not to do. I'm known for the political use of the telephone, but there's a great deal else that we try to do. Sometimes candidates won't buy it, but that's their fault not mine.

You have four ways to contact the voter. You have mass media, visit, telephone, and mail; and the intelligent campaigner uses all four of them in a proper ratio. Some campaigns use only one, or one-and-a-half. Many campaigns

162

never use telephone and mail. Computers are essential in a process that we call targeting, which is the basis for virtually all mail or phone campaigns.

We have four political resources—time, money, manpower, and talent—that are always limited. You spend these limited resources on the four ways you contact the voter—media, visit, telephone, and mail. The computer helps you to decide where to spend these limited resources intelligently.

Now I'd like to tell what I think is the way to win elections. You have a large constituency to start out with, but you end up with two small constituencies when you eliminate, using computers and targeting, all those voters that you can't or don't need to persuade. For example, Matt Reese is a partisan Democrat who will vote the straight democratic ticket, so don't waste time on him except to identify him and get him out to vote if your candidate is a Democrat. The way you win elections is to identify those committed and not voting and get them to the polls. Then identify those who will vote but are not committed and try to win their support.

You have to identify and locate these people first. We grade every precinct within the constituency by three basic things—performance, turnout, and switch-split. Performance will take in demographic factors, size, how they voted in the past, ethnic factors, etc. We'll use the computer to rank them in a range of ten to one. Ten means that we anticipate on the basis of the past that they will perform for our client in the best manner, i.e., high percentages of support.

We compute potential turnout on a ten to one scale also. The large numbers reflect potential, so a high number on this scale means low turnout in recent elections. Finally, the switch-split voter with a propensity to vote one time for the Democrats and the next time for the Republicans, one time for a liberal and the next time for a conservative. They are, of course, the voting but not committed group, and they are very important to us. The propensity to split or switch their ticket is placed on a ten-point scale with ten assigned to those most likely to switch or split.

Using these figures we can list the precincts in order of priority in two lists: for those people voting and not committed (switch-split), the best precinct within the constituency down to the worst; for the people who are committed but not voting (turnout), we list them best down to worst. So we can spend our limited resources down the line until we run out. That way we get the most for our investment. It allows us to list them best through worst in order of potential. It also will allow us to decide what to do in the precinct. Let's say we had a performance grade of eight, meaning very good for our candidate, a turnout grade of eight meaning low turnout, a switch-split factor of two meaning a low propensity to split their ticket. It tells us what to do in that precinct. Using these figures, we decide priority and the best mix of the four types of contact to use to accomplish the objective of persuading and turning out the vote. That's the way we're going to win.

Direct Mail: Campaigning's Sleeping Giant

by Richard A. Viguerie
President
Richard A. Viguerie Company, Inc.

My expertise is in the use of direct mail as it relates to the computer. The political aspect of direct mail over the years has been a sort of country cousin of the more glamorous forms of advertising, such as television and radio. You hear a lot of critical remarks made about direct mail and usually with good cause. I'd say that 95 percent of the political direct mail that I have seen is a waste of money. It's sterile. I'd say with confidence that there are less than eight people in the United States who understand how to intelligently use direct mail as it relates to politics. Contrast that with the many experts who are very competent and have an outstanding knowledge of how to use the other techniques in campaigns. Direct mail is a sleeping giant. There's a tremendous amount of pioneering work yet to be done.

Direct mail is a form of advertising just like television, radio, bus signs, billboards, bumper stickers. It is perhaps the most difficult form of advertising to master because there's a very accurate and precise measure of your returns. In most campaigns, who can say whether what you contributed to the campaign was successful. Maybe a successful campaign was due to your effort or maybe it wasn't. In our work, which I like to think is on a little higher level than some of our cousins on Madison Avenue, we have to live with our returns every day. If I do a mailing on Monday of 100,000 letters that might have cost $15,000, and if a couple of Mondays later $6,000 has come in, I can't tell the client that a lot of people know about him now who didn't before. "Baloney, where's my money?" is the reply.

There is tremendous job satisfaction in this business because we do something one day, and about fourteen days later we can see precisely the results of our efforts.

I have a friend who managed a campaign for a successful congressional candidate several years ago. After the election he said to me, "Richard, I know you make your living in direct mail and that you obviously think it's great, but I wouldn't give you a nickel for all the direct mail in the world. We used it in our campaign, and it was a failure. We went to New York and got a couple of the best people in the television field, and they spent in excess of $100,000 on the campaign, and that was what elected the congressman. We couldn't have done it without these two men and television. We used some direct mail and it was just a bomb."

I said, "Bill, I appreciate that. I know who did your television for you. Who did your direct mail?"

And with a straight face he answered, "A couple of volunteers."

How do you expect direct mail to work when you don't use professionals? You have an amateur prepare your direct mail—an attorney, a doctor, or someone without an assignment in the campaign. But you wouldn't dream of having an amateur do your television. So, no wonder it doesn't work for you in campaigns.

Computer letters have only been in use now about four years; we started in 1965 and 1966. I think I know a fair amount about computer letters, but my knowledge is in the infancy stage compared to what we will know in six to ten years. It's a brand new field, much newer than radio and television.

New Managers for the New Techniques

Putting the Campaign Team Together
By Marvin Gersten

Managing Small Campaigns
By Robert Agranoff

The campaign handler or manager has the single traditional political purpose of ensuring that his candidate wins the election. To this end, the handler bears the overall technical and administrative responsibility for the campaign.

He must retain or hire the professional campaign staff, that is, the campaign specialists and experts who will handle the various technical duties of the day-to-day operation of the campaign. The specialists look to the manager for decisions and guidance, since he, next to the candidate, determines the issue, media, and organizational direction a campaign takes.

There are two distinct types of managers. The first type is the party leader; the second is a "specialist expert" turned manager.

The former type is the most abundant today. They are men who have come up through the ranks from precinct captain to party chairman. Their strongest asset is that they know party and political organization techniques. These techniques, in most cases, enable them to mold an active, unified, and well-controlled campaign.

The latter type, "specialist expert" turned manager, is

more adept at the new campaign techniques of data processing, survey research, media usage, and issue research. He may have been a party regular at some time in the past, but as the manager, he relys on the new techniques rather than the old methods of party and political organization.

Both styles of campaign management exist successfully in the political arena today. In recent years, we have seen an increasing number of campaign managers in whom are combined the skills of the party chairman and the technical expertise of the new-politics specialist. Such men are not only the most sought-after but often the most successful political managers. There is a strong probability that this double-based style of campaign management will become a virtual necessity in handling American campaigns in the future.

The two contributors to this section have had considerable experience in campaign management, and each represents the new double-based type of handler who has both party experience and new politics know-how.

The Honorable Marvin Gersten is Commissioner of the Department of Purchase for New York City. He has been manager of Republican campaigns in New York City, particularly the successful Manhattan campaign for New York mayor John Lindsay. He also managed the campaign of Democratic Congresswoman Bella Abzug.

Robert Agranoff has served as coordinator of 117 Democratic legislative campaigns in Minnesota where he was responsible for securing candidates' access to the new political techniques through the state party organization. He is now a professor of political science at Northern Illinois University and editor of a new book, *The New Style and Technology of Election Campaigns.*

Putting the Campaign Team Together

by Marvin Gersten

Manhattan Campaign Manager
for Mayor John Lindsay

Campaign Manager
for Congresswoman Bella Abzug

I would like to discuss the campaign handler as a handler, not as an advisor, but as someone who gets into a campaign and actually runs that campaign, a man who has to make the decisions about how the campaign should be run, what services we can use and what services we can't.

The new politics, I think, is a misnomer. In many basic ways, even in this electronic age, the old politics still apply. They apply in many instances to the issues and advancements of principles which brought many people, especially the young, into the political process. I think the young were always there. They were there in the forties; they were there in the fifties; they were there in the sixties; and I think they'll be there in the seventies.

I believe very strongly that the campaign team that runs the campaign must effectively manage the campaign and the use of the state party, or the local party system really becomes ineffective. It is very difficult to go to a central point to get your data information, to get your canned commercials, to get the data that you need in the local districts. It just does not work.

I think that a campaign must be run by a campaign manager, and there must be one campaign manager. That campaign manager's responsibility is to make the decisions. You cannot run a campaign by committee. It just does not work. The campaign manager must use professionals. I've worked in several campaigns where these professionals have worked and have done a great job. But the campaign manager, in consultation with his candidate, must establish where that campaign is going, and what is needed to bring the candidate's message to the people.

I believe very strongly in the establishment of a precinct-by-precinct organization. The only way candidates, specifically local candidates from the congressional level down, can get their message across to their constituents is by a door-to-door campaign with the use of the technological advancements we find in the new politics.

When we start a campaign we must look for a great many things. The first thing I've looked for in the management of a campaign is the type of district the campaign is in. The kinds of stands the candidate can take is dictated by the kinds of stands that district will buy. And in identifying these districts, we want to find out which districts we can move.

173

In 1969, we knew very well that the Jewish districts in Brooklyn and in Queens could be moved to vote for John Lindsay. We also knew that the districts in Bay Ridge would never move to Lindsay. In Bella Abzug's campaign we knew that the very conservative districts were not going to be her districts. But we also knew that there was indecision in certain districts.

This becomes very difficult when you have a candidate who is not identified on one end of the spectrum or the other. When you have a very liberal candidate, it's easy. You can look at past records, past gubernatorial or past presidential elections, and past local issue elections. In New York City, we had a civilian review board which told us a lot. We could look to that to indicate what kind of districts we were working in, what kind of pitch we had to give, and what districts we could really move and which ones we could not move. The same applies to the right. It's much more difficult, of course, to identify the middle district and the middle candidates who are really not far to the left or the right.

We have to look at party registration. Will the voters move off the line? There are more sophisticated areas where voters will go from one party to another and back again, and other areas where they traditionally vote the party line. In building a precinct organization, we must use the data to find the swing districts that we must move to the candidate. In many areas, the party system is broken down. Where there is no party organization, you must build one yourself. In building this party organization, of course, it is easier when you're dealing with a candidate who is riding a popular issue. Bella Abzug was a case in point: her district was liberal and against the war. Being a women's liberation person, she had a following. And she has the charisma and style to attract volunteers.

The attraction of volunteers is very important in the political process. These volunteers are not only college students; I think the participation of college students in local campaigns has been overrated. They alone cannot provide the corps for a winning race. Let's not forget the local housewife who has never been active in politics before, who gets turned on to come out and work her block, her building, her neighborhood. The unsophisticated precinct worker is a very effective tool because when local party workers come out and give the party pitch, they're going to vote for the candidate themselves. We used thousands of housewives in this last campaign. It brings to mind the story of a woman who came in to see me and said, "You know, I've only finished three-quarters of my building, but I couldn't finish the rest because my son wanted to take me away for a week to celebrate my 77th birthday."

It is important to bring national issues down to a local level. I've seen candidate after candidate discuss national issues in the campaign but in a way that went right above the voters' heads. They're interested in national issues, but the candidate has to show that he is interested in his district and that he can communicate with the people in his district. How do you do that? When you talk about the war in Vietnam, you relate it to what's happening in the district. When you talk about bond issues that may be on the ballot, you've got to talk about it relating to the district. People are interested in local issues. They're interested in neighborhood schools, in the high price of food, the drug problem. You've got to bring it to them, into their home, because many voters vote on an emotional basis.

Voters really don't know why they're voting for a candidate. They may like him, but much of this may have to do with the media, the media approach, and the literature that comes out. The voters have to have a feeling for the candidate. And they get this feeling from the media.

In campaign management, you have precinct organization, media, advance in scheduling, momentum, negative operations, and, of course, the final election day operations. All of these important for the campaign. When a candidate is scheduled, he must be advanced properly. When a candidate goes into a certain portion of the district, he should know who's there, what the local problems are, and what the feelings of the community are on those local problems. He should make those people feel that he really knows about their district. If he does not do that, he will not get into the gut issues.

A very effective use of direct mail campaigns is the letter that goes to four or five specific districts with specific problems that the candidate can discuss. In one campaign we had an issue involving a specific building that was to be built, about which the people in the area were upset. Four days before election day we sent out a specific mailing tailored to that issue for the precincts surrounding that building. We found out on election day that we did better in those districts than our previous canvassing and polling results predicted. In fact, we did better there than in most other areas.

The personal letter-writing campaign is very important. Personal letter writing is a technique used all over the country. When the campaign starts, we take a list of thousands of local supporters and ask each to do one thing. We gear it to the person who would not come out and work in a campaign

—they never have and probably never will—but want to help. So we ask them for money. We ask them to give us a list of every person they know in the district. We ask them to write a letter, and we give them samples of letters written about our candidate, about why he should be elected.

We write the letter on their personal stationary. We do it on a robo-typewriter so it will be personal, and we have that person sign every single letter personally. So it says, "Dear Joe, I'm writing to you about a friend of mine who is . . ." We hold those letters, thousands of them, depending on the momentum of the campaign, until 10 to 15 days prior to election day, and then send them out into the district. We work on those letters for four to five months. It is a very effective tool, a personal letter, from one friend to another, asking him to vote for a candidate.

It is difficult for a local precinct organization in many instances to effectuate local campaigns. Where national issues are involved, especially gubernatorial or presidential elections, people see the candidate on television, hear him on radio, and read about him in the newspapers. But on a local level, congressional level, or legislative level, many of the voters do not know who is running in their district. They really do not have a sense of participation. Therefore any time a personal approach can be used, whether it be knocking on a door or a personal letter, it has an effect.

Media in local campaigns are very expensive, and most local candidates don't have the money to mount a large media campaign. So we have to try to get as much press coverage as possible. The last campaign in which I was involved I was too lucky; I had too much press coverage. Every time the candidate went on television, it turned off more voters. So we used the negative approach. We cringed every time we saw another newspaperman come up or a television camera roll into head-quarters. We never knew what our candidate was going to say next.

We tried to use literature in order to bring out the local issues. Many say that literature is a tool of the past, but I think that it is a tool of the present. I think that the literature used today is most effective when tailored to local situations. We use certain literature in certain areas. I'm not saying that we use literature in one area to say one thing and literature in another area to say another. We accentuate certain issues that the candidate stands for in certain parts of the district, and other issues in other parts of the district. A very effective theme in the New York campaign was that John Lindsay did the following things for *your* neighborhood. People did not know that he had built this or had done that.

Research is very important. Accurate research will tell what you have done effectively in the local districts. People begin to look at the literature to see if it is just campaign rhetoric. But if they see something that they are personally concerned with, something that they are confronted with, then it works.

Scheduling can be used in two ways: (1) it can be used, of course, to get exposure, it can be used to make news; (2) it also can be used in a negative way, by placing candidates in unfriendly audiences or situations where we know it will be difficult, where we know that he or she will get booed or eggs will be thrown. But such an audience may move those people in the swing districts who have not made up their minds about our candidate. We have used this strategy very effectively by going into awkward situations and trying to

178

create a negative reaction towards our candidate to move voters who do not particularly have a rapport with or feeling for those groups that the candidate faced.

What is a campaign all about? It starts with the voters in the district and the candidate. It starts with the use of media and literature and, of course, the candidate and where he goes. But the thing that goes throughout a campaign is momentum. You build to a climax, you build to election day to get the candidate elected. The momentum of a campaign is very important. Endorsements, local or prominent—should they all be thrown out in one day and forgotten, or should they be paced for the right time to build the momentum?

Sometimes you want to show shifts in voting. In 1969, John Lindsay wanted to show that a lot of the Democratic party was shifting to him. (His campaign manager was one of the best in the business at orchestrating this kind of endorsement.) Every day another major Democrat came out for him, until, of course, the climactic endorsement by Arthur Goldberg was announced. It was very important then.

When do you bring out your local projects? When do you take the negative information you have about the candidate and use it? You can't use it too early; and yet, in some instances, you have to use it early enough so that you can play with it throughout the campaign. But in that momentum, and in that building, you are looking for the gut issue, a gut issue that you can bring from the beginning of the campaign to the end.

What are the attitudes in the district, so that we know how to move: not only who is going to vote for our candidate and who is not, but why are they going to vote for the candidate and why not? We knew very well from some of the polls that Bella Abzug's leftist position on issues really didn't upset many voters, but her personality did upset them. They thought she was too tough, too much like a man; so we knew that we had to tone her down. We also knew in certain areas we had to try to bring her as close to the middle as we could.

I would just like to end with election day, which I think is the most important day of the year. Election day operations are very important. You must bring your voters to the poll. If they sit home, they're not going to count on election night. Regardless of how many people in telephone or door-to-door canvassing operations tell you they're going to vote for your candidate, you've got to bring them to the polls.

In certain areas, it is more difficult; one of the things the computers will show is the type of turnout to expect. Certain areas turn out 20 percent, some 40 percent, others turn out 100 percent. You know that in those areas that are going to turn out 100 percent, you don't have to worry about getting out your vote. You may have to worry about protecting your vote in some of the tough wards in many of the areas in the country, and you make the decision to protect the vote rather than pull the vote.

In many of our areas, we have a very low turnout, for example, traditionally in New York the black areas have the lowest turnout of any areas in the city; but with the pulling operation, going from door-to-door, bringing them to the polls, you can effectively turn out a larger percentage of your vote. Arthur Goldberg ran in 1970 in New York State with a black man on his ticket, a very popular one, yet he pulled less votes in the black areas in 1970 than John Lindsay pulled in 1969.

Managing Small Campaigns

by Robert Agranoff
Professor
Northern Illinois University

As managed by our major parties, American electoral campaigns have traditionally taken the form of door-to-door voter mobilization; that is, direct personal appeal to the electorate by candidates and party workers. In recent years, however, the growth of electoral constituencies and the development of new communications techniques have combined to produce a virtual revolution in campaigning. More and more American electoral campaigns are turning to mass-oriented voter appeals, and thus to print advertising, to the news item, and to radio and television as techniques for influencing votes.

The advent of these new campaign techniques has generated a new breed of professional politician skilled in the financing, planning, and management of mass-oriented electoral campaigns. In the process, the role of traditional party organizations in mobilizing electorates has declined. Professor Frank Sorauf has noted, "As the style of American campaigns turns to mass media, to radio and TV speeches and 'great debates,' and to the arts of advertising and public relations, the political party no longer plays the main role as the organizing intermediary in the campaign."[1] The mobilization of various campaign resources, including financing, is becoming a major responsibility of the new skill groups which the candidate employs. This new campaigning is centered around the formulation of candidate personality appeals rather than appeals to vote for the party ticket or for a candidate as a member of a party. As candidate appeals have increased, party voting has diminished, as witnessed by the increase in split-ticket voting, the large number of minority party candidates elected in constituencies considered safe for the majority party, and the increasing number of candidates elected during a "sweep" by the other party.

The new techniques and the experts who employ them have already had a tremendous impact in presidential, senatorial, and congressional contests, and in gubernatorial and other statewide contests.[2] However, they have seldom been used in local or state legislative campaigns. One reason is that many candidates are simply unaware of the new methods. Still others have reservations about their usefulness. It is undoubtedly true, for example, that candidates for major office deal with large constituencies which lend themselves more naturally to the mass media approach. The legislative candidate, on the other hand, can reach a proportionately larger number of constituents through direct personal appeal. In addition, candidates for lower-level offices are competing for "lower visibility" positions, which means they can expect less free media exposure through coverage by the working press.

On balance, though, it seems clear that the use of the new approach offers impressive advantages in campaigns for lower-level offices, especially at the legislative level where dramatic constituency growth has reduced the effectiveness of traditional campaigning. But a serious problem of implementation remains: few candidates for lower office possess or can afford to buy the high-priced skills and services necessary to mount a full-fledged modern campaign. One solution to this dilemma may lie with existing state party organizations and their proven ability to mobilize financial and skill-group resources. If party organizations were to establish programs of professional campaign assistance, the new techniques might be available to candidates not otherwise able to afford them. Moreover, in the process of managing candidate access to the new techniques, state party organizations would have the opportunity to develop a significant new electoral role to compensate for the decline of the traditional constituency party function.

The purpose of this article is to suggest how a political party organization can acquire and apply the resources and technology demanded by the new approach. It is not a study of individual candidate campaigns, but rather an investigation of the role of a state party organization in a joint legislative campaign effort. As such, it will focus on party efforts to make professional campaign assistance available to legislative candidates.

The Minnesota Experience

During the 1968 legislative campaign in Minnesota, the Democratic-Farmer-Labor party (DFL) designed and implemented a program offering 117 DFL House candidates professional management, assistance of specialists, and access to some of the new campaign techniques. From the opening gavel of the 1967 session of the Minnesota Legislature until election day in November 1968, a professional staff employed by the party organization and a group of specialists in research and media—both volunteer and paid—assisted DFL legislative candidates in their campaigns. The entire operation was coordinated by a professional political scientist experienced in research and campaigning, and familiar with the new approach to campaigning. His staff consisted of five full-time fieldmen and two part-time research-writers.

The DFL's media group consisted of eight working professionals from radio and television, advertising, public relations, printing, and journalism. The campaign research group comprised seven persons with previous research experience, primarily in the areas of polling and data analysis, legislative issues, and legal research. In addition, other full-time party staff members assisted the campaign in fund-raising and technical services.

Though not unprecedented, the DFL's program of campaign assistance certainly represents one of the first efforts by an American political party organization to employ a small number of specialists for the purpose of applying new campaign techniques in a large number of campaigns. The DFL's initial decision to make this effort stemmed from previous campaign experiences. The "stars" of the party—Vice President Humphrey, Senators McCarthy and Mondale, and Governor Freeman—had employed these approaches successfully in the past. But while the party was winning a great number of these state-wide contests, its Minnesota House delegation suffered losses in five consecutive elections. In 1966, only 42 DFL legislators were elected in a House of 135. In a series of post-1966 election surveys, former candidates demonstrated a clear desire to gain access to the types of campaign assistance their partisan counterparts enjoyed in running for higher office. Accordingly, the party organization set out to provide the same type of new campaign services for legislative candidates.

The DFL legislative campaign in 1967-1968 reflected the new campaign approach in three basic ways. First, an effort was made to develop a more "management-oriented" approach utilizing such proven techniques as research, budgeting, systematic long-range planning, data analysis, and polling.[3] Second, recognizing the trend toward candidate-centered campaigns, the DFL's professional legislative staff adopted a policy of supporting the development of candidate organizations and playing down the importance of candidate relationships with the formal party organization within the legislative district.[4]

Third, in response to the increased costs of modern campaigns, the party organization allocated more funds to the legislative effort than it had in previous campaigns. The state chairman and the party's executive committee were committed to raise and spend amounts in excess of six figures for staff and for direct party contributions to campaigns.

In sum, the DFL's 1967-1968 legislative campaign represented an attempt to use a management approach to apply new campaign techniques to candidate-centered campaigns through the expenditure of relatively large sums of money. The dynamics of the process can best be explained by reconstructing the various phases through which the DFL's campaign developed. Sequentially, these phases were as follows: research, candidate recruitment, fund-raising, campaign preparation, candidate training and campaign planning, candidate and campaign cost-effectiveness analysis, and campaign implementation and candidate service.

Phase One: Research

The first stage of the 1968 DFL legislative campaign began with the opening of the 1967 session of the Minnesota Legislature and ran until the legislative candidate search began, some seven or eight months later. During this period the DFL legislative operation was primarily concerned with building cases against GOP incumbents, developing issues for the campaign, and performing election research to assist in campaign decision-making.

The research consultants decided that their most useful effort would be the building of a GOP incumbent "file" for use by DFL challengers. Legislative observers gathered unpublished information on the performance of GOP legislators in committee sessions and in the House's Committee of the Whole. Other volunteers kept complete records on GOP-sponsored bills, developed newspaper clipping files on each GOP legislator, and analyzed legislative roll calls in terms of indices such as party support, liberalism-conservatism, and missed roll calls.

The research phase was also marked by the DFL's first serious attempt to perform computerized aggregate electoral data analysis. The 1966 general election vote from every precinct in the state was recorded on data processing cards and analyzed extensively. The electoral study was designed to help the staff determine priority seats by offering a precinct-by-precinct profile of an incumbent's vote-gathering ability; to determine areas of GOP incumbent strength and weakness, thus suggesting areas from which a DFL candidate might profitably be recruited; to develop campaign strategy and tactics through examination of the data for each precinct in a legislative district; and to allow the party to perform research on its sample ballot, a direct mail technique used to identify DFL candidates in nonpartisan ballot elections.

In the final and critical aspect of the research phase, the professional staff translated the research into a preliminary determination of priority seats for the 1968 election. The basic information used for setting priorities was a combination of "hard" data, including the number of terms an incumbent has served, the electoral strength of the incumbent, and party strength of the district; and "soft" or judgmental information on the electoral strength of the incumbent. The importance of candidate personality factors in Minnesota's nonpartisan ballot legislative elections meant that the potential strength of DFL challengers was assessed almost entirely on such "soft" information as past public service, community standing, and apparent ability to wage a campaign.[5]

This information was translated into weighted quantitative ratings in three categories—incumbent strength, party strength, and candidate potential—and an overall priority ranking of "A," "B," or "C" was assigned for each district. This rating system formed the basis of the candidate recruitment strategy.

Phase Two: Candidate Recruitment

Despite a half century of nonpartisan ballot legislative elections in Minnesota, both major parties have been involved in candidate recruitment for well over two decades. Candidate recruitment in the DFL party, contrary to party practices elsewhere, is not an exclusively local procedure.[6] Thus, the extensive recruitment efforts of the state DFL's legislative campaign staff in 1968 did not represent a fundamental departure from previous practice

However, there were some important strategic changes in keeping with the management approach of 1968. The three-level priority ratings were adhered to rigidly during the recruitment stage and in the campaigns as well. All seats having the lowest rating ("C") were automatically written off as impossible, and no attempt was made to recruit a candidate. If a candidate was recruited for a "C" district by the local party or if a Democrat filed for office on his own, very little assistance would be channeled in his direction. In effect, these decisions reduced the number of candidates to be recruited for non-DFL incumbent seats from 111 to 71.

A second campaign management decision was to involve the professional staff in recruitment more directly and at an earlier stage. Whenever local party considerations would allow it, the party staff personally screened prospects in the field. Their findings were matched against the information used in arriving at priority districts. After staff judgments about the desirability of various candidates, the state chairman and his staff made personal inquiries of prospects concerning their willingness to undertake a campaign. When a preferred candidate was identified, the state fieldman would return to the local area to get the local people to agree that the particular candidate was preferable and to join him in encouraging the candidate to run.

From a management standpoint, recruitment proved to be the longest and most difficult phase of the total campaign effort. It began the day after the 1966 elections, when candidates who lost by narrow margins were urged to make another race, and did not conclude until July 1968, when decisions on the remaining high-priority seats were made final and last-ditch attempts were made to secure candidates for unfilled medium priority seats. In sum, the recruitment process required a significant expenditure of party resources, both financial and personal.

Phase Three: Fund-Raising

Candidates for the state legislature have traditionally received very little money from the DFL party organization. From 1960 on, an additional financial burden was placed on DFL candidates when Hubert Humphrey began to take DFL money outside the state while running for national office. In 1968, party leaders decided that the new campaigning would require substantial contributions from the DFL and, therefore, made a party commitment to raise and expend direct grants of funds to candidates.

Beginning in the fall of the off-election year, the party engaged in the traditional political fund-raising practices of holding dinners, appealing to interest groups for funds, and directly soliciting money from its regular contributors.[7] In keeping with a management-oriented approach, an attempt was made to pool legislative funds for redistribution to candidates on a priority basis. Thus the direct grant of funds and the pooling effort were the innovative aspects of the party's fund-raising program.

Organized labor and the Farmers Union—the long-time sources of party support for DFL legislative candidates—and the House DFL caucus were invited to pool their funds with the party organization and to name a representative from their group to a DFL legislative committee which would participate in strategy and decisions on fund allocation. The House caucus agreed, but the interest groups were reluctant to alter their practice of contributing directly to a candidate's volunteer committee. Thus, a compromise was reached. The interest groups were to contribute a total of $10,000 to the pool for operating expenses. Candidate contributions from interest groups would continue to go to candidates rather than into the proposed fund pools, but the allocation of these funds was the responsibility of a combined DFL legislative committee consisting of representatives from the party organization, the DFL House caucus, labor, and the Farmers Union.

From these various revenue sources, a total of over $200,000 was raised and spent in the DFL legislative campaign. About one-third of these monies was used to defray operating expenses for the legislative program. The remaining sum was used for direct contributions to candidate campaigns. There was a deficit of over $10,000 which the DFL state central committee carried in its regular operating budget. The total revenue and expenditure figure of over $200,000 was impressive by DFL standards. [8]

Phase Four: Campaign Preparation

A substantial number of the DFL candidates were new to party and campaign experience. In addition, many of the more experienced candidates were not familiar with the newer techniques of campaigning. The legislative campaign staff therefore established a candidate training program which emphasized campaign organization and techniques, issue development, and advertising and promotion.

In a more conventional enterprise, the party staff cooperated with the media and research groups in producing legislative handbooks on campaigning, similar to those published by the national party congressional campaign committees. The DFL *Legislators Campaign Handbook* stressed the "how to" aspects of the new campaigning from organization to media. The *House Issues Handbook* was designed to educate the nonincumbent candidate on the key issues of statewide importance. It included research data on GOP incumbents.

The advertising campaign was developed by the media group and by legislative staff members. It was decided to have common advertising, with an identical color scheme and design, in which only the candidate's name and legislative district number would be varied. In addition, the media group decided to develop a general advertising campaign, bearing the name of no particular candidate, urging voters to find out who their DFL legislative candidate was and vote for him.

The entire advertising campaign was organized around a central campaign theme: opposition to the 3 percent sales tax enacted by GOP majorities during the previous legislative session. The GOP governor, Harold LeVander, was to be linked with the GOP caucus and attacked for his failure to keep his promise to oppose any sales tax. The physical symbol was a "Lavender Penny," a purple disc resembling a penny bearing a caricature of LeVander, the designation "Three Cents," and the words "E Pluribus Tax'Em."

Near the end of this campaign preparation phase, most of the DFL candidates had been identified. They were urged to seek endorsements, finances, and volunteer assistance from community leaders, labor and farm organizations, and civic groups at this early stage in their campaigns; to solicit funds from their large contributors; and to enlist their key campaign workers.

The candidate preparation phase marked the midpoint in the party organization's legislative campaign and the beginning of the candidate's campaigns. For the party organization it meant the final wrap-up of the research and the completion of fund-raising events and the candidate search. For the candidate it meant that the decision to run had been made and the task of lining up support just begun. It was now time for the party and the candidate campaigns to come together during the training period.

Phase Five: Candidate Training and Campaign Planning

The fifth phase of the campaign, which stretched from July until Labor Day, focused on transmission of the new techniques of campaigning from the experts to the candidates. Training and planning were necessarily interwoven, because a major goal of the training program was rational campaign planning.

The training period began with a series of candidate workshops. On the first Saturday after the filing closed, all candidates were brought to Minneapolis to discuss campaign techniques—door-to-door campaigning; radio, television, and newspaper advertising; literature and sign preparation;

and other special techniques. The candidates were given a chance to obtain personal advice from media and research experts and incumbent legislators.

This phase of the campaign also featured a series of issue training workshops, held in various parts of the state in order to sensitize candidates to regional concerns. The staff of incumbent state senators and representatives offered basic information about issues and attempted to train new candidates in methods for using or, alternatively, avoiding issues in a campaign. Upon completion of the regional workshops, a single state workshop was held at which more general issues were discussed.

The major emphasis of the training-planning phase was on staff assistance to candidates and campaign organizations through numerous individual conferences between fieldmen and candidate groups. Each fieldman was responsible for approximately 15 of the 71 high and medium priority races. His instructions were to "camp on the doorstep" of each candidate until his campaign was organizationally and strategically planned. Major emphasis was placed on non-incumbents and the six DFL incumbents who were facing difficult reelection races.

The initial step in campaign development at the district level was the establishment of the major campaign committees. The fieldmen first asked each candidate to select members for his general campaign, finance, and publicity committees. The next step was to develop a campaign strategy. Data gathered in the research phase was explained to the candidate, and a written summary of each body of data was provided. The end of this summary suggested an overall strategy, which proposed a proper campaign "mix" of candidate, issue, and party appeals.[9] The information was then discussed in light of the candidate's own perception of the incumbent, his district, and his campaign. The end-product of the discussion was an overall campaign strategy.

After this initial session the candidates assembled their committee volunteers for subsequent meetings with the fieldman to decide on the tactics which would best serve their strategy. At these sessions specific decisions were made on fund-raising events, promotion and advertising, issue emphasis, and candidate image. The physical output of this aspect of the campaign was three important internal campaign documents: first, a weekly campaign calendar which stated the exact day of each campaign event; second, a campaign budget, which projected all conceivable revenue and expenditure; and third, a block-work plan, which pinpointed on a weekly basis the exact area in which the candidate would be campaigning door-to-door. Each of these documents was projected through election day.

Upon the completion of campaign planning as evidenced by the three campaign documents, the field staff returned to their districts to offer technical assistance to candidates and volunteers on the practicalities of campaigning—how to secure a postal permit, purchase envelopes, secure printing, write copy for a brochure, or plan a dinner for a candidate.

This training / planning phase completed the party's task of offering sound management of campaigns. After the experts made strategy, tactics, and techniques available, it was up to the candidate and his campaign group to put forth the most effective effort.

Phase Six: Candidate and Campaign Cost-Effectiveness Analysis

During September 1968, important information was gathered as a basis for allocating scarce resources for the last stages of the campaign. Over the course of the campaign it had become clear that election priorities could not be determined by party strength and incumbent vulnerability alone; the performances of the DFL candidates had to be evaluated before reassessing the initial priority ratings assigned to the districts.

The most important aspect of this information-gathering phase was the independent determinations by the legislative staff of whether the campaign plan was being successfully implemented.

The information gathered was largely derived from the response of the candidate and his campaign workers to questions about implementation of the overall plan, from direct observation of the campaign, and from a check with local party leaders. In addition, the implementation of a candidate's block-work plan was considered an excellent indicator of the individual effort that he was putting forth. Other "collective" indicators, such as local monies raised, were considered as evidence of the effectiveness of the campaign organization.

Unfortunately, information about the campaign and the candidates offers little insight into how a candidate is being received among the voters of his district. Thus, a polling program was established to measure the impact of various campaigns. Scarce resources limited the conduct of surveys to 31 higher-priority districts with questionable status in the "A" or "B" category. A sample of registered voters was drawn, and volunteer interviewers asked questions designed to test voter identification of both legislative candidates; knowledge of party affiliation of both candidates; voting intentions in the upcoming presidential, congressional, and legislative races; reason for voting intention in legislative races; and knowledge of distinguished campaign literature. In addition, an open-ended question asked respondents to identify the major legislative issues.

In general, the candidate and his campaign group were able to use the survey to make assessments about the impact of the campaign and the candidate. The survey information helped local campaign groups measure the extent of voter cognizance of the candidate's party identification effort. In all surveyed districts a rough picture could be drawn of the "candidate image" of both candidates and explanations for projected voting behavior suggested.[10] Finally, the open-ended questions could generate issues for the campaign which had not already been identified.[11]

The survey and field information was also used as a device to exert pressure on reluctant campaigners to accelerate the pace of their campaigns. Candidates were provided further stimulus by the prospect of additional money from the state party coffers in the last stages of the campaign.

*Phase Seven: Campaign Implementation
and Candidate Service*

In the final phase of the 1968 DFL legislative campaign, the staff provided direct services to campaign organizations to help them implement the plans they had adopted. Unlike the earlier technical assistance programs that emphasized management and strategy, these services were designed to make the new techniques of campaigning a realistic possibility for the candidates.

As soon as all the campaign information was gathered from phase six activities, the DFL legislative group met to reassess priority ratings and allocate funds. Very few adjustments were found necessary. In general, each "A" and "B" candidate was to receive some money from the party organization / legislative caucus pool and some from the interest groups. The sums ranged up to $5,000 for "A" priority districts. The "C" candidates received little or no money from the party. Thus in the all-important financial area the priority system of campaign management was carefully followed.

During the final weeks of the campaign the legislative staff made itself available for service on special projects. The office staff assisted in the writing of press releases, speeches, and research reports. The field staff worked with the campaigns on special eleventh-hour problems, including block-working, literature distribution, media advertising, and election day "get-out-the-vote" plans. The fieldmen remained in their assigned districts until election day overseeing the implementation of the campaign plan.

A final legislative activity was the joint publicity campaign. In the last ten days of the campaign, law signs, posters, newspaper and radio advertising, and literature stressed the DFL theme of opposition to the recently enacted sales tax. This candidate advertising program was supplemented by a party program of newspaper and radio advertising.

Another aspect of the joint publicity effort was the sample media material prepared by the party's research and writing staff. These news and advertising materials, in which a candidate could insert his name and local information, included a weekly "canned" press release for radio or newspaper use, bi-weekly radio "spot" scripts, and a series of sample newspaper ads.

With the exception of the fund allocations, these services offered to candidates were not considered a central part of the DFL's campaign. In fact, during this final stage of the legislative campaign, the individual candidates were relatively free to implement the strategies and tactics agreed upon. The funds contributed to their campaigns, the research explained, the issues developed, the services and advice provided were available for the candidates and their groups to incorporate into their campaigns. It was left up to the candidate-centered groups to implement strategy by employing the new techniques which were now made available to them.

Conclusion

In 1968 the DFL party was more successful at the polls than it had been in five previous elections. Instead of suffering losses, 15 new DFL House members were elected. Six other DFL candidates were defeated by margins of 151 votes or less. One cannot, of course, prove that the new approach to legislative campaigning caused this reversal in party fortunes. To be sure, many factors, including the appeal and effort of the individual candidates, contributed to this success. On the other hand, it is important to note that this change in party fortunes was concomitant with a recognition by party organization leaders that the nature of the party organization's role in the electoral process was changing.

The organizational role of political parties in the electoral process is declining in importance because of two interrelated factors. First, as recent research has indicated, party voting is diminishing in importance while voting for "the man" and the issues surrounding him appears to be on the rise. [12] Second, newer and more sophisticated means of appealing to voters are being developed. The candidate poll, the television spot, the computer letter, and the computerized precinct priority system are all predicated on selling *the candidate* and his carefully researched issue positions to the voter. These two trends reinforce each other, rendering campaigns and voting less party-centered. While a good deal of the evidence for those trends appears to be derived from the more dramatic presidential, senatorial, and gubernatorial races, it is only a matter of time before other candidates begin to mount similar appeals through the mass media. This is because constituencies are getting larger, the new techniques are becoming better known, and candidates at all levels are increasingly aware of the decline of party voting.

If political parties are to remain a significant force in the electoral process, it seems clear that they will have to develop a role more in tune with the new candidate-centered campaigns. The Minnesota experience indicates that parties *can* play a central role in modern campaigning by making the new technology available to candidates who could not readily acquire it. In addition, other state party organizations in the United States, the Republican and Democratic National Committees, and the national party organizations in Britain are beginning to assist their candidates in the new campaigning. [13] Thus, candidate consultation and technical service have emerged to bolster previously existing programs of financial assistance. [14] These new programs are far too recent, however, to identify a trend. Indeed, the available evidence indicates that very few party organizations have systematically pursued the new campaigning.[15] Many state parties appear to be in a transitional stage in which there is less emphasis on the traditional door-to-door "party vote" mobilization but very few initiatives in other directions.

If party organizations were to embrace the new approach to campaigning, they might well recapture some of the control they have lost over the electoral process. When party leaders are made aware of the political implications of change in technical and electoral behavior, they can respond to the challenges by forging a new electioneering role. The 1968 DFL campaign ponts in this direction and suggests how this role might develop in the future:

1. Parties will play a greater role in the management of entire campaigns. As they begin to offer such wide-ranging and specialized services as budgeting, computerized aggregate electoral data analysis, polling, advertising assistance, and even the development of comprehensive door-to-door plans, they will get into the critical areas of strategy, tactics, and day-to-day management.

2. Parties will require the services of a variety of experts. In order to provide a comprehensive package for lower-level candidates who cannot readily gain access to these skills, parties will have to acquire the services of consultants in such diverse areas as campaign management, advertising and public relations, media production and allocation, polling, issues research, and electoral data analysis.

3. Regular party staff will have to be skilled in interpreting and applying the new technology of campaigning on a day-to-day basis. Due to time and cost factors, lower-level candidates will not ordinarily enjoy regular contact with

campaign consultants, but they will have to have access to someone skilled in the preparation of advertising copy, the pretesting of a poll, or the interpretation of computer print-outs of election statistics in the field. Party employees can fulfill this role though it will inevitably mean that the important skills for professional party work will be less inter-personal and more technical in character.

4. Parties will have to make a substantial commitment to, and investment in, different kinds of research. The new campaigning is highly oriented to using the methods and findings of behavioral research in voting behavior, legislative behavior, polling, management science, advertising, and publications. In order to meet this challenge, party organizations will have to alter the direction of their research operations toward research for candidates, at the expense of the traditional "issues" research, which is so often based on the development of the public image of parties rather than candidates. Under such programs, parties would be responsible for the creation and maintenance of data sets and data bases on precincts, census tracts, legislators, and voters for usage at campaign time for planning candidates' strategies, appeals, and image-building.

5. Campaigns will be more expensive and will require greater financial commitments on the part of central parties—national, state, or metropolitan—for candidates in small constituencies. The available evidence indicates that central parties have not given a great deal of financial assistance to these candidates.[16] If parties are to facilitate access to the new campaigning, they will have to provide the services of consultants, perform research, and make direct grants for media acquisition. All this is more expensive than

the local party volunteer-oriented, old style of campaigning. It will have to be done at the central party level because local constituency parties simply do not have the financial or managerial resources to do the job.

6. As party campaigns become more expensive, and as the scale of party campaigning increases, political parties will have to become more management-oriented and more cost-effective. The cost of using consultants, using media and advertising, and employing a staff will be so great, relative to what party leaders have previously experienced, that parties will have to initiate practices and make decisions unfamiliar in most lower-level campaigns. For example, the wise allocation of resources may require the writing off of many contests, even to the point of not fielding candidates. Campaign management devices, such as tight scheduling, block-work plans, budgets, and cost-effective devices like polls and the DFL's field-testing procedures, will have to be utilized as a matter of course in lower-level campaigns.

7. Lower-level campaigns will begin to require fewer persons and different skills. Mass media approaches and personal campaigning do not require the manpower needed in the older style of campaigning. Traditionally, the chief recruiting ground for party workers was the local party organization—the largest single repository of persons likely to support a candidacy. As campaigns begin to use more radio, television, direct mail advertising, and other types of candidate contacts with voters, the need for party loyalists to mobilize party votes will diminish. What the lower-level candidate will need is a group of personal loyalists who are amenable to the new technology of campaigning and are willing to provide the organizational and financial underpinning

for such an endeavor. As far as the formal party committee at the local level is concerned, it will become less useful in providing the electioneering services which are required by the new politics.

8. Efficient implementation of campaign plans, utilizing priority systems, will ignore the traditional area-neighborhood plan of party organization. In the DFL plan, the electoral data were used to determine the order of priority of block working and for direct mail advertising. In other campaigns similar studies have been used to determine the proper "media-mix" for the entire constituency. Once the priorities are set, implementation no longer depends on the availability of party workers in the neighborhood, or the willingness of the local party to purchase advertising materials. Rather, workers are assigned to areas on a priority basis without regard to area availability, and the use of media is determined by priority factors such as "impact" and "reach." In this scheme of campaigning the important boundary lines are not counties, wards, or precincts but newspaper, radio, and television markets, available address files, and zip codes.

9. All the preceding trends will reinforce the development of candidate-centered campaigns and accelerate the declining role of traditional local organizations in electioneering. The plain fact is that, under present circumstances, local parties are not offering needed campaign assistance because they simply are not geared up to perform such services. Nor is it conceivable that a great proportion of local constituency parties will acquire the wherewithal to meet this challenge.

10. The same trends in campaigning suggest a new role for political parties above the local constituency level. The

1968 experience of the DFL offers evidence that state party organizations can become significant and highly powerful agencies in candidate-centered campaigns. Other parties at the state level and the National Committees are beginning to recognize that modern campaigning requires a different type of service from the party organization and are beginning to take the necessary steps to provide it. If the trend continues, the state, national, or metropolitan parties could become managers of congressional, legislative, and other campaigns and thus play a vital role in the electoral process. In the long run, such events could conceivably contribute to a shift in party power from the local to the central level. As candidate-centered groups realize that the central party organization is the meaningful agency in winning elections for them, allegiance will shift toward that body and its resources.

The DFL effort to make some of the new techniques of campaigning available to its legislative candidates represented one of the first attempts at providing such a comprehensive package of research, technical assistance, and finances. During a time when political party organizations are losing their hold on electioneering, the DFL experience suggests that parties might continue to play a role in this vital aspect of politics if they recognize the value of providing sophisticated new services.

Future campaigns in the smaller constituencies will always be faced with the problems of marshaling sufficient resources for a campaign based on the new techniques. Nevertheless, in an era of declining importance of party—both as a symbol which motivates voters and as an organizational force in mobilizing votes—candidates will increasingly be called on to mobilize their own voters, using their own appeals. In the absence of a pre-existing party sentiment, candidates will be forced to manufacture favorable sentiment toward themselves, using the new techniques, for they must get their messages across to a large number of people in a short period of time. The problems of mobilizing resources for the new techniques and of a party role in campaigning may both be alleviated by a new form of party participation in campaigns.

[1] Frank J. Sorauf, *Political Parties in the American System* (Boston: Little, Brown, 1964), p. 108.

[2] Herbert E. Alexander, "The High Costs of TV Campaigns," *Television Quarterly*, V (Winter 1966), p. 48; Herbert Alexander and Kevin L. McKeough, *Financing Campaigns for Governor: New Jersey, 1965* (Princeton: Citizens Research Foundation, 1969), pp. 28, 52; Edward C. Dreyer, "Political Party Use of Radio and Television in the 1960 Campaign," *Journal of Broadcasting*, VIII (Summer 1964); Heard, p. 367; Robert King and Martin Schnitzer, "Contemporary Use of Private Political Polling," *Public Opinion Quarterly*, XXXII (Fall 1968); Frank J. Sorauf, *Party Politics in America*, (Boston: Little, Brown, 1968), p. 242.

[3] John F. Becker and Eugene E. Heaton, "The Election of Senator Edward W. Brooke," *Public Opinion Quarterly*, XXXI (Fall 1967); Dan Nimmo, *The Political Persuaders: The Techniques of Modern Election Campaigns* (Englewood Cliffs, N.J.: Prentice Hall, 1970); James M. Perry, *The New Politics* (New York: Clarkson N. Potter, 1968); Ithiel de Sola Pool, Robert Abelson and Samuel Popkin, *Candidates, Issues and Strategies* (Cambridge, Mass.: M.I.T. Press, 1965).

[4] Sorauf, *Political Parties*, p. 108.

[5] Charles R. Adrian, "Some General Characteristics of Non-Partisan Elections," *American Political Science Review*, XLVI (September 1952), p. 776.

[6] Frank J. Sorauf, *Party and Representation* (New York: Atherton, 1963), Ch. V; John C. Wahlke, Heinz Eulau, William Buchanan, and LeRoy C. Ferguson, *The Legislative System* (New York: John Wiley, 1962), p. 48.

[7] Herbert E. Alexander, *Responsibility in Party Finance* (Princeton: Citizens Research Foundation, 1963), pp. 10-31; V. O. Key, Jr., *Politics, Parties and Pressure Groups*, 5th ed. (New York: Thomas Y. Crowell, 1964), pp. 498-499.

[8] Prior to 1968 only a few thousand dollars was directed to candidates for office, at any level. See Robert Agranoff, "The Minnesota Democratic-Farmer-Labor Party Organization: A Study of the 'Character' of a Programmatic Party Organization" (Unpublished Ph.D. Thesis, University of Pittsburgh, 1967), pp. 303-304.

[9] Lewis A. Froman, Jr., "A Realistic Approach to Campaign Strategies and Tactics," in M. Kent Jennings and L. Harmon Zeigler (eds.), *The Electoral Process* (Englewood Cliffs, N.J.: Prentice Hall, 1966); John H. Kessel, "A Game Theory Analysis of Campaign Strategy," in Jennings and Zeigler.

[10] Angus Campbell, Gerald Gurin, and Warren E. Miller, *The Voter Decides* (Evanston, Ill.: Row, Peterson, 1954), pp. 52-65.

[11] For an account of how polls are used in the development of campaign strategy, see Becker and Heaton, pp. 352-358; Louis Harris, "Polls and Politics in the United States," *Public Opinion Quarterly*, XXV (Fall 1961).

[12] Phillip E. Converse, Warren E. Miller, Jerrold Rusk, and Arthur Wolfe, "Continuity and Change in American Politics: Parties and Issues in the 1968

Election," *American Political Science Review*, LXIII (December 1969), pp. 1083-1105; Milton E. Cummings, Jr., *Congressmen and the Electorate* (New York: The Free Press, 1966), pp. 31-46; Donald E. Stokes, "Some Dynamic Elements of Contests for the Presidency," *American Political Science Review*, LX (March 1966), pp. 19-28.

[13] *E.g.*, Alexander, *Responsibility*, p. 43; Democratic National Committee, *Democratic Campaign Manual, 1970* (Washington, D.C.: 1970); Republican National Committee, *Electronic Data Processing for the Political Executive* (Washington, D.C.: 1967); Richard Rose, *Influencing Voters* (New York: St. Martins, 1967).

[14] Kevin L. McKeough, *Financing Congressional Campaigns* (Princeton, N.J.: Citizens Research Foundation, 1970).

[15] Robert L. Chartrand, "The Role of Automatic Data Processing in Politics," paper presented to the Midwest Regional Vote Workshop, American Heritage Foundation, Detroit, Michigan, May 1967. A revised version of this paper will appear in Robert Agranoff (ed.), *The New Style and Technology of Election Campaigns*, to be published in 1971 by the Holbrook Press.

[16] *C.f.*, Alexander, *Responsibility*, pp. 31-37; Donald G. Balmer, *Financing State Senate Campaigns: Multnomah County Oregon, 1964* (Princeton, N.J.: Citizens Research Foundation, 1966), pp. 33-39; Robert J. McNeill, *Democratic Campaign Financing in Indiana, 1964* (Princeton, N.J.: Citizens Research Foundation, 1966), p. 28.

Ethics
of the
New
Politics

Loaded Guns and Other Weapons
By James M. Perry

And What About a Hitler?
By David Broder

A Brief History of Dirty Politics
By Samuel J. Archibald

Are the new politics ethical? Do the techniques of the new politics increase communication between candidate and voter, or do they give the politician greater ability to manipulate the electorate? These are the questions dealt with in this section, and all three contributors have come to similar conclusions: the techniques of the new politics are themselves not unethical, nor are those who use them necessarily manipulators. Like most other aspects of life, the new politics can be used for better or for worse, depending upon all parties involved.

Three journalists and political analysts have addressed themselves to these questions. James M. Perry is a political columnist and reporter for the *National Observer*. He is the author of one of the first comprehensive books about the new techniques, *The New Politics: The Expanding Technology of Political Manipulation*, published in 1968.

David Broder is a political reporter and columnist for the *Washington Post*. He has worked for *Congressional Quarterly*, the *Washington Evening Star*, and the *New York Times*. He is co-author of *The Republican Establishment* and contributor to *Politics and the Press*, the first book in the

University of Maryland's Distinguished Lecture Series.

Samuel J. Archibald is a former journalist, having worked for the Associated Press, United Press International, and the *Sacramento Bee*. As special assistant to Congressman John Moss (D.-Calif.), he helped to write the Freedom of Information Act of 1967. He is a freedom-of-information consultant and assistant professor of journalism at the University of Missouri, and executive director of the Fair Campaign Practices Committee.

A number of questions about the ethical implications of the new politics remain to be answered and will have to be explored in future conferences and further discussions. Two of these questions ought to be raised here.

The first has to do with money. The new political techniques, including television and computer time, are expensive. Will dependence upon these techniques for election success in the future mean that only rich men or candidates with wealthy backers will be assured political victory in our system?

The second question has to do with talent. The new political techniques require special talents of political candidates, and these talents may not necessarily be those useful in political decision, administration, or statesmanship. The candidate who uses television must be telegenic; he must have a new kind of charisma; a sense of showmanship gives him a great advantage. Will dependence upon television mean that we will have actors for politicians, movie stars and sports heroes in the Congress, and "show biz" characters as our future statesmen?

Certainly, these kinds of questions need further debate and exploration.

Loaded
Guns
and
Other
Weapons

by James M. Perry
Political Reporter and Columnist
The National Observer

Political campaigns in America are not sponsored by the Ethical Society—not now, not ever. We have a phrase for unethical campaigning: "Dirty Politics." It has been a problem since George Washington's time. It will still be a problem long after Charlie Guggenheim has spliced his last tape.

The idea of a political campaign, a campaign manager might suggest, is for one candidate to win, the other to lose. It's a contest. And because the human animal is combative, nasty, and ill tempered, the temptation to cheat a little is as strong in politics as it is in poker.

We can't legislate ethics. We can't even create workable guidelines.

We tried once, you may recall. Following the 1950 election—a classic sink hole—Senate subcommittees headed by Paul Douglas and Guy Gillette examined ethics in government and especially in political campaigning. Both concluded that it would be helpful to have some kind of a committee or a commission to examine political conduct. The outgrowth of these recommendations was the Fair Campaign Practices Committee.

The committee has written a code that it distributes to candidates in each federal election. Candidates who sign it pledge themselves to "campaign in the best American tradition," "to uphold the right of every qualified American voter to full and equal participation in the electoral process," "to condemn the use of personal vilification and character defamation," "to condemn any appeal to prejudice based on race, creed, or national origin."

The key section says: "I shall condemn the use of campaign material of any sort which misrepresents, distorts, or otherwise falsifies the facts regarding any candidate, as well as the use of malicious or unfounded accusations against any candidate which aim at creating or exploiting doubts, without justification, as to his loyalty and patriotism."

Amen.

Remember those guidelines. Now let us consider a couple of television commercials that appeared in the 1970 election.

Vance Hartke vs. Richard Roudebush. A Roudebush commercial. The image on the screen shows a military rifle being handed from one person to an actor playing the role of a Viet Cong soldier. The voice-over intones: "The weapons the Viet Cong use to kill American servicemen were given to them by Communist countries. . . . Senator Hartke voted for the bill to permit American trade with those countries.

Isn't that like putting a loaded gun in the hands of our enemies?"

Talk about loaded guns!

The Hartke people filed a complaint with the Fair Campaign Practices Committee. The Roudebush commercial, they said, was in clear violation of the code.

Not so, said the Roudebush people, relying on truth as a defense. Hartke voted against an amendment by the late Senator Dirksen to prohibit the providing of assistance to Communist countries.

Sure enough, said the Hartke people, their senator voted against that amendment. But it was a terrible piece of legislation, and just about everybody voted against it.

The Hartke people concluded: "Today we have a situation in which the Republican candidate for the Senate not only accuses Senator Hartke . . . of questionable patriotism but goes so far as to charge him with contributing materially to the deaths of young Americans in Southeast Asia. . . . [It is] shocking and unprincipled."

The Roudebush commercial was, in fact, outrageous. It was one of the worst of its kind I have ever seen.

But who shall judge?

I am sure there are those who really believe that Hartke's voting record permits such an indecent statement. Those people, I suppose, would be rock-ribbed, God-fearing, straight-ticket, right-wing Republicans.

Let's go back a little farther in time to another commercial. 1968. Democrats vs. Richard Nixon and Spiro Agnew. Joe Napolitan, the Democrats' media man, produced a spot that put the name "Agnew" on the screen and then filled the sound track with the roar of a man's laughter.

CBS' Mike Wallace, in a news special aired October 20, 1970, asked Napolitan about it. "Now," said Wallace, "what about the morality of that? After all, this fellow was running for the Vice President of the United States. You may disagree with him, but do you ridicule a potential Vice President? Or President?"

Napolitan: "Well, I guess we did. I don't know whether it's proper or not."

Mike Wallace: "Yeah, that's what I mean."

Napolitan: "If I had thought it was improper, I wouldn't have done it."

So, who shall judge?

I am sure that there are those who deeply believe that Agnew was, and is, such a caricature of a human being that ridiculing him that way is fair sport, even, perhaps, a public service. These people, I suppose, would be rock-ribbed, Nixon-Agnew damning, straight-ticket, southpaw Democrats; or, perhaps, "pragmatic" image-makers.

All of which is to make the not terribly original point that what is one man's broth is another man's poison.

Thus, it seems to me, *institutional* judgments on campaign ethics are not very workable. The Fair Campaign Practices Committee, I might note, doesn't make such judgments (although, in 1970, it introduced an arbitration procedure). If it did make judgments (Richard Roudebush is a dirty campaigner), its supporters couldn't deduct their contributions, and that, of course, would be fatal. So all the committee does is provide a forum to air grievances.

Some will argue that such a forum isn't enough. They would say we should have tougher measures to deal with tougher problems. Especially NOW—and here's the point—

when we have been buffeted by the introduction of all these subliminal and subtle techniques to woo and manipulate the poor, gullible voter.

Well, the techniques of political campaigning have changed, and I like to believe that I was one of the first political reporters to chronicle those changes.

I think we can safely say that the television set and the computer are both here to stay. The wonder of it is that politicians took so long to discover them. And that journalists took so long to discover that politicians had made the discovery.

The conventional wisdom tells us that television and the computer are subtle in their impact; that TV is subliminal—subtle and subliminal, I suppose, like Roudebush's spots and the Agnew commercial.

The fact is that no one quite knows how television works on the human mind and the human emotions. What evidence we have suggests, in fact, that television reinforces beliefs and judgments already held. And that the print—newspapers, by God—are more apt to sway opinion.

This dismal chasm in human knowledge has not prevented Joe Napolitan or Harry Treleaven or Roger Ailes or Charlie Guggenheim from putting all the rent money in the tube. It hasn't prevented Joe McGinniss from telling us how Richard Nixon was "sold" to us in 1968.

We have, I think, panicked in the face of a technique that may not work in quite the way its partisans have contended.

I think I can state an aphorism: A candidate cannot win a closely contested *general* election relying just on a television blitz. He needs more. He needs to be personable and convincing himself. He needs at least one credible issue. He needs a good staff, good polls, good organization. And, finally, it's nice to have a bit of luck.

Further explanation: sometimes, a candidate can win easily in what should have been a closely contested *primary* election with a television blitz. In a primary, the communications channels aren't so cluttered with other peoples' messages. The target—the audience—is smaller. A saturation campaign is possible, at less cost. This kind of campaign works especially well when the opponent is either asleep or indigent, or both.

And it works best with a good (which is not to say admirable) issue. Joe Napolitan blitzed Pennsylvania with his candidate, Milton Shapp, running against the "machine" in the Democratic primary in 1966. Forget that the machine was rusting in, say, the Bronze Age; forget too that Shapp tried—and failed—to get the machine's support. The issue caught on, and Shapp's opponent failed to respond. In Texas this year, Lloyd Bentsen blitzed Ralph Yarborough. Bentsen attacked Yarborough as soft on God, prayer, mother, country, and law and order. Yarborough woke up too late to respond effectively. And Bentsen's performance so impressed the Nixon strategists in Washington that they adopted Bentsen's primary tactics for general elections in almost every corner of the nation. But what worked for one man in one primary failed to work for many men in many general elections. Praise be.

What I'm suggesting is that even the Great Unwinking Eye of television has its limitations as a campaign tool. Right, Harry? Right, Roger? Right, Charlie?

The success of television as a political tool could be further limited if political reporters paid a little more attention to it.

I believe that every political spot commercial should be covered in the same way as every major speech, every major press conference, every major vote by a political office-holder or political candidate. I mean stories should be written that say: "In a 30-second spot commercial introduced on local television stations last night, Candidate X charged that his opponent supports the Viet Cong."

Thereafter, in the same story, the opponent should be allowed to reply. One presumes his reply would take the form of a denial.

The unfortunate truth is that most daily newspapers in the United States don't begin to cover political campaigns. I would make a special exception of David Broder's *Washington Post*. From the *Post*, I learned that Sam Grossman's campaign in Arizona was fading long before I heard anything about Joe Tydings' troubles in Maryland. In fact, I never did hear much about Tydings' troubles. And, as a result, I lost the office pool.

To get back to the point: too many newspapers believe it is enough to take press releases from the candidates, write a headline, and toss them into the hopper. In states as large as Texas, newspapers don't assign reporters to follow their major candidates. It is, I think, a scandal.

Journalists are conned all the time. Take polls, for example: Oliver Quayle leaked more polls this year than he took, it seems. I remember a leaked poll—not Quayle's—that had Nelson Gross leading Pete Williams in New Jersey. And the news—news, it was judged—was printed, in the final hours of the campaign.

I think newspapers should refuse to print anything about a poll unless a reporter has had an opportunity to determine its validity, one way or another. Who took the poll? What was the size of the sample? Was it a telephone poll? If the poll is going to be published somewhere else, well, then, explain the poll's strengths, its weaknesses. Be skeptical.

All of this requires that political reporters know something about polling. Too many of them don't. They should learn.

Ethics in politics is involved here. I have found that politicians and campaign managers will manipulate anyone, anytime, if they can get away with it. I don't blame them. That's their job. It's my job to refuse to play the game.

There are other obvious things that could be done. Final-hour political advertising should be refused by newspapers, television, and radio stations. A last-minute charge is almost always a phony charge.

I think radio and television stations should give more live coverage to political campaigns. I think reporters should be sharper and more sophisticated. I think radio, television, *and* newspapers should give a great deal more free time and free space to political advertising.

Given this, and more, I think we can live with these new techniques.

Using television to sell a candidate like television had been selling products for years caught a lot of people by surprise. It was a new weapon—like the English long bow. But everybody knows about it now, and there is, I suspect, a backlash by the voters to the more outrageous extremes in its use.

The reaction was exaggerated too, I suspect. Joe Mc-

Ginniss can be held partly responsible for that. Television doesn't have mystical or magical qualities, and the results in November tended to prove it.

It is probably true that the use of *free* television is more critical than *paid* television in forming voters' attitudes. There's more and more of it available. Robert Ailes, Roger's brother in REA Productions, reports that Thomas Meskill, one of their clients, was offered more free time in Connecticut than he could really handle. That's a good sign.

But doesn't paid television open the door to the smear and to dirty politics in general? Of course it does, but maybe not in a way that is singular. The spot commercial is a kind of sloganeering, and we've always had that. I'm not at all certain I would favor the elimination of spot commercials. To do so, it seems to me, is artificial; it is almost unnatural. What we would be saying is: it's all right to dissemble and simplify with Alka Seltzer but not with Nelson Rockefeller.

The computer has opened new doors too. Thanks to the computer, literature can be mailed to almost any group on almost any subject, quickly and easily. A new twist this year was the computerized mailing of thousands of "telegrams" to voters. It's a gimmick that should be exposed for the fraud that it is, but I'm not convinced we should stay awake at nights worrying about it.

The computer, like television, simply makes it easier for a candidate to communicate with the voters. In itself, there's nothing wrong with that. We should condemn the abuses, not the mechanisms.

There was testimony recently before the House Ethics Committee, in which Representative Morris Udall's suggestion that all spot television commercials be banned was somewhat typical. Representative John Anderson suggested that spots be limited and that the federal government pay for longer television programs.

I'm not sure I agree with all this.

To sum up briefly: we have developed new political techniques that at one time were frightening to many of us. We've lived with them for a while, and now they don't seem quite so terrifying—not to me, anyway. The techniques aren't as manipulatory as we thought they might be. At the same time, the voters have turned out to be a little more sophisticated than some of us had thought they would be.

But these techniques are expensive, and there is simply no way to run a complete campaign without them.

So, now, we're getting to the final question, which is not so much ethical as it is moral.

The real question is money. Jess Unruh is right: money is the mother's milk of politics. And these new techniques demand so very much money.

To me, it is simply immoral that Nelson Rockefeller can outspend any rival by margins of four- and five-to-one. It happens every four years. And every four years he wins. A Rockefeller campaign is what the new politics is *really* all about—unlimited money that leads to television, radio, computers, a huge and expert staff, polls, pamphlets, advance men, press releases, airplanes, buttons, hats, telephones. Everything. Each in its place.

A Nelson Rockefeller campaign is one of the Seven Political Wonders of the World. I forget what the others are.

As my children regularly say to me about almost anything, it isn't fair. IT ISN'T FAIR.

A caveat: it is true that money alone does not guarantee

success. It is not just Rockefeller's money, but also the fact that so many people think he has been a pretty fair governor. And consider Nelson's brother, Winthrop. Someone told me that Winthrop spent more than $30 for every vote he received.

But, all things being fairly even—and things weren't at all even in Arkansas—money does talk.

No one can win without *some* money. And, thanks to television and these other techniques, *some* money now means *more* money.

Good people aren't running because they know they can't honestly raise the money they would need. More and more rich men are running, because they can.

There are no easy answers. Things are so bad we can't even get legislation that would tell us, with reasonable precision, how much money candidates are spending. We can't even discover the dimensions of our problem. A reasonable accounting of campaign spending is a necessary first step—and such an obvious one. And we can't take it.

We must demand honest accounts. Thereafter, we must find ways to reduce the odds that now favor rich men—not to eliminate the advantages of the rich man—we'll never do that—but to cut his odds.

We are perilously close to having a political system that is a sham for a democracy. That is immoral. That is tragedy.

And
What
About
a
Hitler?

by David Broder
Political Reporter and Columnist
The Washington Post

As you all know, journalists' confidence on any subject is inverse to their knowledge of the subject; and if there is anything we know less about than politics, it is probably ethics. But when I considered the others who might talk about this topic—politicians, pollsters, and campaign managers, for example—I decided probably a journalist would be the right choice after all.

There was an implication in the invitation that we were supposed to be the moralizers in this discussion and tell how sordid the whole business of the new politics really is, how unethical its manipulation. And I fell to that task rather enthusiastically, since moralizing gives you almost as warm of feeling inside as liquor can. But I found somewhat to my chagrin that I really couldn't work up a good case of moral indignation. I began to worry why.

So I went back to James Perry's book, *The New Politics.*
And I reread his description of the frightful prospect of a
presidential campaign of the future where the candidate
would be, and I quote, "moving from state to state with a ro-
botlike precision, being fed the data from the polls and the
simulator, while behind the scenes manipulators contrive to
elect him, little caring whether he may or may not be qualified to be President of the United States."

It reminded me of a conversation I had at a lunch shortly
after the 1964 election with some people who were involved
in devising the media campaign for the successful presidential
candidate that year, a man named Lyndon Johnson. They
described, with what I can only call lip-smacking glee, the
way in which they had foisted on the American public a picture of Barry Goldwater as the nuclear-mad bomber who was
going to saw off the eastern seaboard of the United States and
end everyone's social security benefits. At the end of an almost sensual description of how they had manipulated and
maneuvered all this, one of them apparently thought that an
ethical comment was called for. "The only thing that worries
me, Dave," he said, "is that some year an outfit as good as
ours might go to work for the *wrong* candidate."

Recalling the arrogance of that remark and the perils of
which Jim Perry warned us, I decided I was going to try to do
some hell-raising with the practitioners of the new politics.
But I found my efforts were impeded by the memory of what
I had read about the campaigns of the preelectronic period.
An earlier philosopher named John Dewey wrote back in
1927 about the politics of that era, a time when he said parties were "not only accepted as a matter of course, but popular imagination could conceive of no other way by which offi-

cials (might) be selected and governmental affairs carried on." He explained why this system of politics, why old politics, if you will, was so ruinous from every point of view. He talked, first of all, about its effect on the voters.

He said of the voters: "Instead of being individuals who in the privacy of their consciences make choices which are carried into effect by personal volition, we have citizens who have the blessed opportunity to vote for a ticket of men, mostly unknown to them and which is made up for them by an undercover machine in a caucus whose operations constitute a kind of political predestination. There are those," he said, "who speak as if the ability to choose between two tickets were a high exercise of individual freedom. But it is hardly the kind of liberty," he said, "contemplated by the authors of the Constitution."

Then he talked about the effect of the old politics, his contemporary politics, on issues. He said, "Since the end of the Civil War, practically all the more important measures which have been embodied in Federal legislation have been reached without a national election which turned upon the issue and which divided the major parties. American party politics seem at times to be a device for preventing issues which may excite popular feeling and involve bitter controversies from being put up to the American people."

Finally, he made an observation about the effect of this kind of politics on the men who were involved, the politicians themselves. He said, "As a rule, what decides the fate of a person who comes up for election is neither his political excellence, nor his political defects. Only exceptional candidates get by on the basis of personal responsibility to the electorate. ... The tidal waves swamp some, the landslide carries others into offices. Habit, party funds, skills of managers of the machine, [those evil men!], the portrait of a candidate with his firm jaw, his lovely wife and children, and a multitude of other irrelevancies, determine the issue."

Now this was the old politics. So I asked myself, "What is there really fresh to be indignant about in the new politics?" The technology of the new politics in itself is clearly not evil. What grounds really are there to object to computerized mailings as opposed to hand-addressed and hand-stuffed envelopes? Is it a more dehumanizing process? I don't think anybody who has ever sat at one of those card tables stuffing envelopes would think that it was inhumane to let the machine take over that part of the burden.

Is the new politics depersonalized, really? Is a candidate more remote or less when he comes into a home via television than he was when he came by radio or when his words were recorded in the cold type of the newspaper?

Is polling data a danger to the candidate? Should he be denied the knowledge of the issues which his constituents are concerned about, their present knowledge and feelings about those issues?

On the contrary. I think we saw in the 1964 campaign with Senator Goldwater what can happen if a national election is wasted on what are really settled questions in our politics, an election in which a President of the United States can carry the vote in the state of Tennessee, for example, by saying, "I will not sell Tennessee Valley Authority." We paid a price, I would contend in all seriousness, for that kind of irrelevant campaign. We paid a price because the issue that was really before the country that year—the Vietnam War—was never talked about substantially in that campaign. We had to wait four years before we even began to address that subject.

If there is a case to be made for giving the candidate data on what the voters' concerns are, what their opinions are, what the state of their knowledge is, then we clearly must grant him the freedom to use that knowledge as he wishes. Indeed, it seems to me that in all this preoccupation with the technology of the new politics, we overlook the point that all we are doing is beginning to apply to a public function—an important public function—techniques that have long been available and used for less important private functions in commerce and industry.

The new politics is systematic politics. It is rational politics, in the application of resources to a problem. It seems to me it is, in the fundamental sense, real American politics, because it is our boast that we have learned how to manage enterprises in this country. If we are learning now finally to apply some rational techniques of management to the campaigns and to the election of candidates, it seems to me that it would be foolish to condemn that development as unethical.

I come back to the question, "What should be the proper source of indignation about the new politics?" I thought of the hardest kind of case that had ever been put to me, a case that may be hypothetical, of an ambitious young man who employed a team of advisers to analyze his personality, his views, and then find a district where the constituents' tastes and interests matched his personality. And then, according to this story, he moved to the district and prepared to run for office. That sounds pretty contrived, and it raises the fascinating question of what happens if there is a redistricting; does he have to change his personality at that point? But really, is that more objectionable in ethical or moral terms than the cases with which we are all familiar of a rich man in effect buying himself a nomination in a state or district? I decided that it was probably not the purposeful matching of voters to candidates that was objectionable.

Is the objection that the new politics prevents people from understanding the real character of the candidates? I didn't think that I could sustain that charge either, because television biographies and other techniques probably give people at least a little clearer picture of the men and the women who are running for office.

Is the objection to the new politics that it keeps the focus off the issues? That would be a serious charge if it were a sustainable indictment, but as I think the quotation from Dewey indicates, serious men 50 years ago, before there was an electronic tube, before there were computers, made the same kind of objection to the politics.

It seems to me that it is possible to argue, at least in some cases, that the new techniques have facilitated an understanding of the issues. I would submit that the voters of Tennessee in 1970 were probably exposed to as intensive a dose of new politics as any voters in the country. And they probably knew more about the way in which candidates in that senate race had voted on at least on some of the questions that had come before the Congress than most voters in most states ever hear about.

Well then, what is the problem, really?

One very serious problem is that the new politics costs an awful lot of money. The way campaigns are financed now makes that cost an extremely dangerous problem for this country. It is probably not true in literal terms that you can buy an election. But the lack of money can deny men an opportunity to compete. In the state of California this year, I am told, a handful of men made it impossible for a candidate for governor to compete for the office to which he had been nominated. The technology of the new politics runs up the costs of a campaign, but the problem of financing a campaign would probably be there even if we were running old politics with today's inflated prices. And we have to face up to the problem of campaign finances—disclosure, limitations, and public funding—as a compelling problem in itself.

The other problem of the new politics, the ethical problem, is one that is not very often alluded to. The new politics makes us realize something that is fairly uncomfortable: the marginal role that politics really plays in the lives of the American people. Somebody said that television commercials are really most effective with the indifferent voter, and that, I think, is the key to the situation.

As Dewey suggested 40 years ago, if the public was really involved in politics, a lot of what happens in a campaign would not only be irrelevant but would be truly dangerous to a candidate. An informed electorate would probably punish a candidate who resorted to the typical kind of oversimplifications that are used in many of the campaigns we saw in 1970. There would certainly be no need for vast expenditures to establish name identification in politics.

But the fact is that the voters are disengaged; they are disenchanted with politics. And the reasons for that disengagement and disenchantment were there before the new politics and the new techniques came along. They go back, I suppose, to the question of what happens in a society of 200 million people when there is a loss of a sense of community, a

227

one particular ideological way, I don't think it is arguable lack of connection between the activities of the rulers and the problems of the ruled. Now if the new political techniques are adding to that sense of alienation, then I think, they bear a very heavy burden. But that's a proposition we have to examine. And here I would really like to come to the ethical question, "What if Adolph Hitler could command the services of the new politics?" Well, I would presume that if a modern-day Hitler arrived on the American political scene, he would find that campaign management talent was available to him and if he decided, on the basis of the research that his researchers provided, that anti-Semitism was a good issue, it would not be impossible for him to use that as an issue in his campaign.

The more serious question is, "What happens after that?" I think the assumption that is made in most of the proposals for clamping down on the new politics is that bad politics drives out good. Cheap politics—in moral terms, not in financial terms—really undermines responsible politics in this country, the proposition goes. Well, I would like to suggest that that is a proposition we really ought to question.

In my own view, the evidence can be mounted just as effectively on the other side of that argument. Now here we have to become fairly subjective in judging who is the good guy and who is the bad guy, what is responsible and what is irresponsible in politics. I would certainly not make the argument that the better man has always won. But I would put forth two propositions that I hope are realistic, not pollyannish.

One, I would argue that the techniques of the new politics have been used, and used effectively, across the political spectrum and have not biased the outcome of our elections in that these techniques have predetermined the outcome of the election for one side—conservative or liberal, Republican or Democratic—as against the other.

Second, I would suggest that the voters have shown considerable ability to discriminate between candidates on what a reasonable man might describe as quality standards in campaigns which have been dominated by the new politics.

Quite the contrary from cheap politics undermining responsible politics, it may be the case that in today's technology and competition, good candidates may force the bad candidates to come up to their own level, and good politics may make cheap politics ineffective politics.

What do I mean by that? I mean that a candidate who is effective in unstaged circumstances as well as in staged circumstances may shame an opponent who can act effectively only in staged circumstances. I think we have seen that in some recent elections. I think that a candidate who can respond honestly to the concerns that the voters feel may have a real advantage over one whose answers are contrived, mechanical, and false. I think we've seen that happen.

At the risk of utter heresy, I would even suggest that there is some reason to think that a political party which has vigorous leadership, strong cohesion, a strong sense of competence and direction, may have an advantage in an election over one whose record in office fails to inspire confidence about its governing capacity. I think we've seen that in some recent elections.

For all these reasons, I don't honestly feel I could argue that the new politics is responsible in any fundamental way for the problems we have in this country. Political problems we have—plenty of them. But we are deluding ourselves if we think they stem from the techniques of the new politics.

A
Brief
History
of
Dirty Politics

by Samuel J. Archibald
Executive Director
Fair Campaign Practices Committee

I've handled a part of 200 campaigns in 1966, 1968, and 1970, the part which involved "dirty politics" or complaints of dirty politics. The question of whether the new politics is or is not dirty often revolves around the ethical problems of political advertising. Of course, there is one medium which, to be effective, requires short and simplistic slogans; one medium that requires a dramatic use of visual techniques, color, and impact. There is one medium which is impossible to use for the discussion of issues. Its best use is for sloganeering. It lends itself to unfair campaigning. I refer, of course, to billboards, thus making the point that dirty politics is not new, nor is the new politics necessarily dirty.

The dirtiest campaign we've had in this nation was the campaign between Grover Cleveland and James G. Blaine in

1884. The slogan of the Democrats against Blaine was that he was the "continental liar from the state of Maine." The slogan against Cleveland was "Ma, Ma, Where's my Pa? Gone to the White House, Ha, Ha, Ha," referring to his bastard daughter.

This campaign, incidentally, was a fine example of the backfire of dirty politics. A Protestant minister in New York City created a slogan, "Rum, Romanism and Rebellion." It wasn't in 1928 in the Al Smith campaign that this was used first. It was first used in New York City, but its effect was not what the minister had planned. It made the large group of Irish Catholics in New York City mad. It backfired. It made them mad enough to vote for Cleveland, giving the state to the Democrats, and probably the Presidency to the Democrats for the first time since the unfortunate occurrence in 1861-1865.

This backfire effect is what the Fair Campaign Practices Committee is all about. We serve as the channel through which the backfire against dirty politics can be used, by enforcing and promoting a Code of Fair Campaign Practices. It is an effective code, in spite of—or maybe because of—the new political techniques.

I don't think there's anything really new in political garbage. In each campaign year of 1966, 1968, and 1970, there were some 505 campaigns in which the issue of dirty politics was raised and handled by the Fair Campaign Practices Committee. These are the races for President, for Congress, and for governorships. During these three election periods, we received the same number of complaints about dirty politics every year. About 13 percent of the races bring in complaints about dirty politics. Complaints come from different districts. We don't have the same clientele every time. The timing has been the same, however. About 40 percent of the complaints come in the last week of the campaign. The area where dirty politics is most prevalent has remained the same. New York wins the dirty-politics prize with more complaints than from anywhere else. The Midwest comes in second, the West third. The South and border states file the fewest complaints, maybe because they finish their dirty politics in the primaries.

In the 1970 campaign, we had more complaints about unfair television advertising, but, of course, there were more advertisements on television than ever before. Therefore, the complaints increased in about the same proportion that television political advertising increased. There was more poll manipulation in 1970, but there was more use of polls.

The 1970 campaign ended with an example of the old style of dirty politics, not the new politics. A newspaper advertisement was run in 70 some newspapers against eight senatorial candidates. Using big, black type, the ad called the candidates "radicals and extremists." Every one of the eight candidates this ad was supposed to help, upon being contacted, repudiated the ad. Seven of the eight candidates attacked by the ad won. Dirty politics, old style or new style, doesn't pay.

The Code of Fair Campaign Practices condemns appeals to prejudice based on race or religion. In 1966, 18 percent of the complaints about dirty politics were on race and religion issues. In 1968, only 9 percent were about race and religion. In 1970 only 3 percent of the complaints were about race or religion. This is an encouraging trend, but we will never remove racial and religious issues from politics. All politicians make racial and religious appeals, and this is not necessarily unfair. If Senator John Stennis were a Negro, he wouldn't be elected from Mississippi. If Bella Abzug were a WASP, she wouldn't have been elected from the lower east side of New York City.

We received more complaints in 1970 about dirty politics on television. Any communications system that extends the reach of a candidate's voice and permits more people to see him can be used by demagogues, dirty politicians, and other candidates. Of course, more people hear an unfair attack, and more people see an attractive phony when he stands up on a soap box or when he buys television time. The medium itself is not necessarily dirty. It's only dirty when it's used by guys who do dirty things.

If television and the television manipulators had been around in 1920, I can just imagine the sort of campaign they would have mounted. They would probably have elected some handsome man, with a nice smile and no brains. They probably would have presented somebody who liked poker and women but who was always featured on the tube as a homebody on his front porch. If we'd had television in 1920, do you realize Warren G. Harding would have been elected President?

My conclusion is that new politics is not dirtier than the old politics. V. O. Key, Jr., said that dirty politics created a sort of Gresham's Law of politics. His comment applies today, and it will apply through the 1970's. He said, "Those who promise the most for the least will, in the long run, drive reasonable and just men from public life." This applies to the old politics, and it applies to the new techniques.

The Fair Campaign Practices Committee only moves

into a campaign when asked; we only get involved when we receive a complaint. The candidate, the manager—the political experts—must decide whether or not complaining about dirty politics and using our facilities is going to help or hurt them. There were, for instance, many news stories about questionable tactics in the Senate race between Senator Vance Hartke and Richard Roudebush in Indiana. But we received only one complaint from Hartke. A television ad showing a Viet Cong soldier receiving a rifle from someone was accompanied by a voice-over saying the guns used to maim and kill American boys result from Senator Hartke's vote permitting trade with Communist countries and concluding: "Isn't that like putting a loaded gun in the hands of our enemies?" We set up an arbitration system in 1968. Senator Hartke asked for arbitration during the 1970 campaign. We asked Roudebush if he would agree to arbitration under the rules.

We informed him we would turn the case over to the American Arbitration Association, if he agreed, but Roudebush refused to arbitrate. Under our rules, all we could do was notify Hartke that Roudebush had refused to arbitrate and was in default. Hartke could have used this as a beautiful publicity weapon to beat Roudebush around the head and shoulders. He did have one press conference, but it was ineffectual.

We received a similar complaint in the Utah senatorial campaign between Senator Frank Moss and Lawrence Burton. The same thing happened: Burton refused to arbitrate. The same message was sent to Moss as was sent to Hartke, but Moss set up a major press conference announcing Burton's refusal to arbitrate. In effect, he said that fair campaigning, like apple pie and motherhood, is a good thing and he's for it. He pointed out that the committee said Burton would not arbitrate and said he obviously was unfair. This press conference, run by the governor of Utah, received major coverage. The fair campaigning issue was a campaign issue from then on. The complaint of dirty politics served, according to the Moss people, as a most important issue for them. They ended the campaign with this issue, and they feel that it made a major difference in their campaign.

How long does it take from the time we get a complaint until the time we act upon it? It depends upon the period of the campaign. In the last week of the election it can take five days. In the last weekend it can take five hours. In the early part of a campaign we take as much time as we can use.

An appeal to the Fair Campaign Practices Committee, filed after the Friday before a Tuesday election may, itself, be dirty politics and will be publicly rejected if what is complained about happened earlier than the previous week. Certainly, there are last-minute dirty politics that come up, candidates complain, and we do handle it. If, however, the candidate could have complained earlier, then we reject it. We've asked the information media to adopt just this same sort of procedure for their advertising. In previous years we received many last-weekend complaints about new attacks made too late to answer; this year there was only one complaint in that category. Apparently, much of the media adopted the same system.

The main value of a complaint—some people say the only value—is the publicity value. People like fair play in politics just as they like fair play in sports, and publicity about dirty politics is effective. We collect the facts from both sides and provide the information to the press corps in Washington. Publicity of the complaint and publicity of the answer is the result. And it works—it works if you believe the democratic system, based on an informed electorate, works.

What
the Future
Holds

What Will Be New in the New Politics?
By Ithiel de Sola Pool

Alienation, Protest, and Rootless Politics
in the Seventies
By Robert E. Lane

Edmund Burke observed, "To complain of the age we live in, to murmur at the present possessors of power, to lament the past, to conceive extravagant hopes of the future, are the common dispositions of the greatest part of mankind." In this section two eminent students of political science avoid these pitfalls. Their analysis of the present puts to rest many of the widely accepted statements about politics and gives us a new perspective on the future.

Ithiel de Sola Pool is professor of political science and a member of the senior staff of the Center for International Studies at the Massachusetts Institute of Technology. His field of major interest is public opinion and communication. He has been a leader in the development of techniques by which detailed projections of public opinion can be made through the simulation of attitudes and attitude changes on a computer. In 1959, Dr. Pool and his associates founded the Simulmatics Corporation for the application of simulation methods. His technique was used for election studies during the presidential campaigns of 1960 and 1964. His results are described in his book *Candidates, Issues and Strategies.*

In his chapter, "What Will Be New in the New Politics?" Dr. Pool clears away the underbrush of what is not new in politics and then gives us a view of politics in the wired city with many television channels permitting a rebirth of the specialized audience and with two-way "demand media" beginning to replace mass media.

Robert E. Lane is professor of political science at Yale University where he specializes in public opinion and the election process. He is the author of *Political Life: Why People Get Involved in Politics, Political Ideology,* and co-author of *Public Opinion.* He is 1970-1971 president of the American Political Science Association.

In his chapter he explores the impact of media on the politics of those who are alienated, protesting, or rootless. You may be surprised to find yourself among those he describes.

What Will Be New in the New Politics?

by Ithiel de Sola Pool
Professor of Political Science
Massachusetts Institute of Technology

As we look two years into the future, the best prediction that we can now make is that 1972 will be a pretty conventional election. There are such things in American politics as "critical elections," ones in which there is a major realignment of the electorate that lasts for some substantial time thereafter. Walter Dean Burnham has just published an outstanding book on such elections (Burnham, 1970). The last such election was that of 1932. The main thesis of this paper is that no such major change in American politics is now going on or is likely to occur in the near future.

Many are the commentators who believe that the American political system is decomposing before our eyes. Television commercials, Weathermen bombings, computer simulations, the defeat of long-time incumbents, and the hair styles of the young are all somehow thrown together as evidences that the good old ways are gone forever, and that American politics is something that it has never been before. There are those who think that the new trend is a conservative or Republican majority. There are those who think that the new trend is revolution. There are those who think that the new trend is manipulation by professional managers for hire. The only thing that they all agree on is that it is new. And to some extent they are inevitably right, for it is the nature of man's life on earth to be ever changing. But to recognize that there is change is not to admit that all of the sensational statements about the purported changes are correct, nor to fail to recognize how slow and sluggish changes in human institutions generally are.

The term "the new politics" is an unfortunate one. It means many things to many people. Terms that label intellectual trends by time and place rather than by content—e.g., New Left or Americanism—suffer from this defect. New politics is a star example, and it is likely to be applied to any political fact that is perceived as being a change.

To some the new politics is a monster spawned on Madison Avenue. Our conference program says: "The 'New Politics' has been the big news of the 1970 political campaigns. The political scene of 1970 is being reshaped through a combination of mass media, sophisticated public opinion analysis, and computers."

That is a good statement of one legitimate view, but a view from which I must enter a partial demurrer. It singles out for attention three changing elements of politics: mass media, opinion research, and computers. What I should like to try to do is to assess just how fundamentally these changing elements have changed American politics.

Of these three the most important in its effects on politics is clearly the use of mass media, and most recently of television. Even if commercial television in this country (and earlier commercial radio and a commercial press) had no other effect on politics at all, its effect on the costs of campaigning has been massive. The rise in the expense of running for office has been one of the more regrettable recent changes in American politics. How serious this trend is and how widely it has been recognized are illustrated by the fact that the association of campaign consultants recently called on the Congress (unsuccessfully) to override the President's veto of the bill imposing a ceiling on television spending in campaigns.

There are other effects of television on the character of American politics which are less easily documentable than its effects on campaign spending. It is widely believed and perhaps true that a different kind of personality comes across well in the living room than in street parades and rallies. In 1952 when television had reached only part of the electorate, we found that Eisenhower's and Stevenson's personalities came across differently depending on whether they were seen on television or aired over radio (Pool, 1959). There are such things as television personalities. However, almost no solid research has been done on the personality factors for television effectiveness. We have only the hunches of the pros, and they are rather vague.

It is also widely believed that image-makers have acquired unprecedented powers because of the manipulative techniques available with the television camera. The *New York Times* quotes Dan Seymour, president of J. Walter

Thomson, the world's largest advertising agency: "I get scared when I look down the road as to what can happen; it's pretty frightening in what it forebodes for the future—you can pack the House with a bunch of nincompoops." There are reasons, however, for being a little bit skeptical of the power of television. It is undoubtedly effective in speeding up the formation of new images. With 60 percent of the American public watching material mostly from three networks any particular night, a featured story dealing with something on which the public had no previous images will have a profound effect. An excellent treatment of such impact is found in Lang's study of the 1952 convention coverage (Lang and Lang, 1969). However, well-established attitudes are not changed that easily. Major campaigns, which are the ones that can afford television, deal mostly with already familiar figures and with topics about which strong predispositions already exist. That is less true in the primaries, which, therefore, is where the television blitz is most apt to be effective.

Furthermore, in a competitive situation where both sides have access to the airwaves the net effect of television may be minimal. The dangerous power of television exists in the situation where access is one-sided.

Finally, the alarm expressed by the media is somewhat affected by their overestimate of their own effectiveness. If one looks back to the literature on propaganda after World War I, one will find many similar alarmist theses about the magical powers of the hidden persuaders of that era and the ease with which they could mold whole populations. Careful research, such as the studies of election campaigns (Berelson, 1954), showed a very different picture, one of a fairly intractable population not easily moved from its fixed prejudices.

Much of the alarmist literature had come from the practitioners of advertising themselves, who quite sincerely vastly overestimated their own effectiveness. So it is today with the television experts commenting on their own selling of candidates.

So we may assess it as true that the rise of the mass media has vastly increased the cost of campaigning, and that it has speeded up the process of initial image formation, but it is probably not as true that it has created a powerful device for brainwashing. Even more important is the fact that whatever has been happening for the past century is about to be reversed in some important respects.

The basic dynamic of the mass media revolution was that it became increasingly cheap to get multiple examplars of the same message to ever larger numbers of people. The invention of the printing press was the first step in that direction. Radio and television pushed the process of centralization further because of the shortage in the number of channels on the spectrum. In the case of television, most people had to watch one of three or four alternative messages; those who sent those messages had an enormous guaranteed audience. The emergence of UHF slightly changed that situation, but only slightly. What is about to change it in the next two decades is the new technology of communication based upon the wired city and the computer. In the visible future the average home will have 20 to 40 wide band communication channels instead of 4 or 5. Also the audience will have the capability of communicating back so as to request responsive information. Voters will be able to dial into a reference source for facsimile or other feedback that is responsive to the matters about which they are curious. In an environment where such "demand media" have begun to replace mass media, candidates will not be able to rely solely on slick spots in prime time. The wired city is likely to produce a pattern on television much more like that on radio today with its talk shows and specialized channels. The mass audience may be to a large extent atomized. With decay of the dominant networks, politics is apt to become once more dependent on effective political organization to overcome the individualistic character of media use.

Those, however, are not trends of the immediate future. 1972 may be the most canned television campaign of history, but if so, it will probably hold that record forever. The only thing that will prevent it from being that is if the Congress legislates to restrict television budgets and spot political commercials. However, shortly after 1972, multi-channel cable television will begin to cover a significant portion of American homes, and it will not permit the kind of canned television campaign which is arousing such disquiet today.

In general I have concurred that there are complex new trends in politics arising from the media revolution. Now let us evaluate the other alleged trends arising from professional campaign management, namely increased use of opinion research and of the computer.

Polls, it is true are now used by politicians. However, political polls are not typically very sophisticated. The first scientific election polls were made in 1936 by George Gallup and Elmo Roper. In that year the *Literary Digest* flopped with an unscientific postcard poll of tens of millions of voters drawn from telephone and automobile registration lists. It predicted a victory for Alf Landon who on election day actually carried two states. In contrast, Gallup and Roper did well with their couple of thousand scientifically selected respondents each. That put the polls in business. However, it was not till 24 years later, in 1960, that polls came to play a visible part in the management of a national election campaign. That is the length of time it takes for human institutions to adopt new practices. No presidential candidate until John Kennedy and Richard Nixon used polls seriously. Franklin Roosevelt and Harry Truman had no use for egghead presumptions challenging their intuitive grasp of politics. Dwight Eisenhower did not see the point either. Adlai Stevenson, an intellectual in politics, understood polls, but found it incompatible with his moral posture to the guided by them. In 1956 in particular he chose a strategy that flew in the face of all the research advice given him. The polls showed foreign policy to be Republican terrain, but he decided nonetheless that the right thing to do was to advocate a nuclear test ban. He went down with colors flying, and in so doing perhaps laid the groundwork for the adoption of such a policy by a later administration, but not his own.

By 1960 a new generation of politicians had come of age, comprising men who had grown up on the polls. They were empiricists and "new politicians" in the sense of the word that we are now using. They were both avid readers of polls, and Kennedy at least, I can personally testify, was an acute interpreter and critic of the data. Lyndon Johnson too used polls eagerly. In that respect it is fair to talk of a new aspect of politics beginning in 1960.

But polls, even if now used by virtually all major politicians, are not very important in most campaigns. In the first place good polls cost money, and most politicians lack money. In the second place, most politicians still do not know how to use polls; they do not know the right questions to ask, or how to interpret statistics. Not many politicians have social science training. Partly for those reasons, and partly for others, the average politically sponsored poll is most charitably descried as mediocre in quality. There are some good, sophisticated, careful ones with appropriate questions and well-drawn samples. They are the exception. It is common to find polls done by volunteers, or based on 200 to 300 cases, or done with obvious bias in the questioning. A survey of surveys to find out what proportion of political pollers have dared to predict that their client would lose would be both revealing and embarrassing.

As for computers, it is true that they are now widely used for such routine purposes as preparing canvassing and mailing lists, typing form letters, bookkeeping, and tabulating previous votes or current surveys. They are not used for strategic management or even sophisticated analysis. In 1960 a simulation model was used by the Democratic party to make survey analysis dynamic. The Republicans are currently toying with simulation ideas and may use a simulation in 1972, but my guess would be that there will be a longer lag before serious simulation research is used by political parties—perhaps not 24 years, but more than 12 years after the 1960 proof of the feasibility of a strategic campaign simulation.

In general, if by the new politics one means that professional technicians in advertising and opinion research are taking over campaign management and displacing the part time amateurs and "pols" whose regular jobs are in law, real estate, and similar fields, then there is clearly something to the assertion of change. Professional campaign consultant firms are growing in number and activity (Rosenbloom, 1970). However, those campaign consultant firms are mostly small, marginally profitable, and constantly on the edge of collapse. Politics is not a good business. It has its excitements and attractions that lure men to it who could make a better living in other ways. The specialists who are thus drawn in may slightly improve the technical quality of the information efforts of candidates, but their efficacy is easily exaggerated.

Nonetheless there are trends towards greater professionalization of campaign services, greater expenditures on media, and more skillful use of research for campaign management. If one were to project the trends of the past decade for two more decades, then there would be good reason for concern. These trends are partly good and partly bad, but carried far they certainly would create serious abuses of the campaign process. However, the linear projection of trends is a dangerous business. Growth does not go that way. It continues to a certain point and then stops, checked by countervailing processes of maturation. In this article we shall try to take account of factors that seem to promise a reversal of direction of some of these trends. There are good reasons to believe that by 1972 the television blitz will have reached its peak and will begin to be subject to measures of restraint—perhaps by then, perhaps shortly thereafter. There are also reasons to believe that we shall see no marked increase in the efficacy of manipulation. But before we start speculating about the future, let us look at other current trends that are referred to by some commentators as part of the concept of the new politics. These include a supposed trend toward ideological politics, issue politics, or participant politics.

By its more sympathetic partisans, the new politics is described not so much in terms of media manipulation by professional technicians as in terms of a disenchanted electorate looking for new and more meaningful ways to make politics responsive to its needs. Unfortunately, that which its more romantic partisans describe as the new politics, in this sense, is neither new nor is it politics.

Sometimes the new politics is said to be a newly awakened concern of the voters with issues. It is also described as a feeling of alienation by the voters from established political institutions and from the politicians. It is described as participant politics with the involvement of the young and the poor in the processes of political life. If any or all of those is what one means by the new politics, then it is not new because it is a myth. There is no substantial reason to believe that any of those things are happening.

There is no substantial evidence to suggest that the voters are more concerned with issues today than they were 20, 30, 50, or 100 years ago. I must concede that there is also no substantial evidence to indicate that they are not more concerned with issues. Candor requires that we admit to an almost complete lack of objective evidence either way on this question. Twenty or forty years hence we may be able to establish a trend by comparing 21st-century social-science studies of voters making up their minds with the pioneering studies that have been conducted during the past 30 years. Perhaps eventually current research will find patterns quite different from those described by Lazarsfeld, Berelson, and Gaudet in their study of the 1940 election (1944) or in their subsequent studies (Berelson, 1954) or in those by the Survey Research Center (Campbell, 1960). But to date, if there has been any change since 1940 in the extent to which voters attend to issues, it is not sufficiently strong to be demonstrable. In a few minutes I shall qualify that remark, but for the moment let it stand as a reasonable first approximation.

Also one must question the notion that alienation and disenchantment with politicians and the political process are new or growing. No more venerable or orthodox American political cliché exists than the statement that "all politicians are corrupt," unless it be the mother's notion that "I didn't raise my boy to be a politician." True, every male baby was thought to be potentially a future President, but if he were not to be President, certainly no self-respecting, ambitious lad would look forward to a lesser role in politics. The research is not at hand for any firm documentation of trends, but studies of the prestige of occupations have not shown politicians to be a profession of declining prestige. The profession of politics never had much prestige (Reiss, 1961), and if anything, that has risen (Janowitz, 1958). A country founded on the principal that "that government governs best which governs least" can hardly be thought to have once idolized politicians.

It does seem to be true that in the short run there has been growing disenchantment with politics as measured by responses to public opinion poll questions about the political scene. Phillip Converse has documented that (1971). However, that finding may easily be interpreted as a fluctuation reflecting the undoubted fact that Franklin Roosevelt and Jack Kennedy had personalities better able to arouse mass enthusiasm than did the other three presidents of the present political epoch. There is no reason to assume that because we have seen less charisma for the past seven years (since Jack

Kennedy's assassination) than before then, that the age of charismatic presidents is past.

It is easy to misinterpret current generational differences and assume that because the young express more discontent with society and with the political system than do the old, that we are launched on the crest of a wave of growing alienation. The young are indeed more discontented; the young and the old differ relatively little in most political views, but one of the few items on which consistent differences are found is expressed disenchantment with the status quo. However, unlike such generational shifts as decreasing anti-Negro prejudice among the young, which will presumably persist and thereby cause a gradual change in national attitudes as the age cohorts march on, the difference in contentment with current institutions between the young and the old is apparently a phenomenon of aging. It is always there. The young are always more radical, and as they get old, they make their peace with existing institutions. In short, the conflict of the generations is a complex phenomenon. It is important to sort out which current differences between young and old are phenomena of aging and which are phenomena of generational change between cohorts. There is no evidence of a generational wave of alienation.

Certainly if there were a trend of increasing alienation, one could hardly simultaneously postulate a trend of increasing citizen participation. There is some eivdence for the hypothesis of increasing participation. Among the data that can be interpreted that way are the trends in voting participation and also the rise in educational levels and in the size of the middle class. A careful analysis of that data is not my subject today. However, it is appropriate for me to note that

251

these changes are not new but rather are very slow, long-run changes that have been taking place throughout the whole century. Furthermore, the rise in participation was mostly from 1920 to 1952 and may not have continued since then. By 1952 participation had returned to levels that had been normal before the 20th century. Furthermore, the change in the shape of the social pyramid does not mean that there is more political participation by the young or the poor, even if there is more participation in total. The growth in middle-class reform movements, voluntary associations, and political activities may reflect only the growth of the middle class, leaving the poor much where they were in level of activity. Indeed there is some reason to think that the decline of the slum political machine, of militant trade unions, and of immigrant foreign language ethnic organizations may have decreased the political options of the poor, although it is true that these trends are simultaneously being offset by the rise of communal organizations among newly mobilized strata of the poor, specifically the Blacks and the Chicanos.

In short, if the new politics means, as it does to some, either issue politics, or alienation, or participant politics, there is no real reason for believing that any such new politics is newly with us.

On the other hand, it would be naive to believe that nothing new is happening in American politics. There are important changes. The most important are the decline of the political party and the simultaneous rise of electronic media of communication. That is what I would like to talk about today.

The theses that I am developing here are not novel. Political scientists will recognize similarities with the conclusions reached by Burnham (1970). Nor is what I have to say based upon detailed microanalytic research. Surprisingly, however, political scientists in the search for the nonobvious have often neglected the most obvious aggregate indicators. What I am here trying to do is to note some of the broadest aggregate facts and their implications as a context that must be taken into account in further analysis.

The decline of political parties is certainly changing American elections, though that trend is rather poorly labeled "the new politics." It, too, is a very long-run and gradual change that has been taking place fairly steadily since 1932 and with some anticipation before that.

In the half century or so of which 1900 was the center, the heart of the American campaign process was precinct organization. A large literature describes how, particularly in American cities and particularly in their ethnic ghettoes, ward committeemen commanded precinct captains who made it their business to know every voter personally, to arrange patronage jobs, to distribute Thanksgiving baskets and coal in winter, and thus to build around themselves a party organization. The active members would join together in a club. It was that organization that turned out the vote on election day. The only mass media then widely available were newspapers, and they played an important role; but the party organization was more effective, especially among the less literate voters.

The growth and functioning of such party organizations provided the subject matter for a large and important sociological literature. Lincoln Steffens wrote dramatically and descriptively at first hand, while M. Ostrogorsky and Max Weber analyzed the rise of the tightly disciplined party caucus, describing it as one of the most significant phenomena of modern society. They recognized that demagogues or charismatic "politicians by vocation" could organize the newly-mobilized masses through party organizations. They believed that by so organizing the masses, the charismatic demagogue helped to maintain the stability of mass democracies. Indeed Lenin, looking at the party machines in Germany and America, had the illusion that the disciplined party of professional revolutionists that he was advocating was merely a transfer of modern practices to backward Russia; he thought that he was mimicking those political machines.

Ironically, the disciplined mass party which Europe thought it was imitating from American politics never evolved in America to nearly as disciplined an organization as the social-democratic parties of the Continent. Still, by contemporary standards, the American turn-of-the-century machine was quite powerful.

The start of the decline of the American political party can be dated from the Pendleton Act and civil service reform in 1883. That reduced the spoils of office. Acceleration of the party's decline can be attributed even more to the rise of two competing modes for organizing the populace: the bureaucratic welfare state and the mass media.

At first glance one might characterize Franklin Roosevelt as the architect of a great new national Democratic party organization, for in 1932 in one of the few critical elections in American history, he turned a long-term Republican majority into an equally long-term Democratic majority; he created a new political alignment around the New Deal. However, whether he knew it or not, the virtuoso politician, Roosevelt, was thereby eroding the very party system that he manipulated so well. By providing social welfare through bureaucratic, nonpolitical channels, he did more to break the power of American political machines than any reformer ever had.

Franklin Roosevelt, an ambitious man and a consummate politician, acted to destroy the traditional Democratic party machines, not just inadvertently, by social policy, but also quite consciously in order to create a national power structure of his own, independent of the collection of baronies that the urban machines were. As Governor of New York he had fought with and broken the power of Jimmy Walker and his Tammany machine. All through his administration he had to cope with the liability of such machines as Mayor Hague's of Jersey City. He also found the then radical programs of the New Deal up against solid opposition by the nation's press. To meet these challenges of competing power centers, Roosevelt developed a national style of personal leadership based on charisma and on the use of the new medium of radio.

Radio played a major part in national politics for the first time in the election of 1928. For the first time the great majority of the American public could have an almost first-hand experience with the candidates. Most voters heard the voices of the candidates in that context speaking to them.

Just as automobiles, when first introduced, were made to look like carriages, so the radio speech, when first introduced, was simply the traditional campaign rally oration. Roosevelt, however, recognized the distinctive character of the medium and invented a package specifically designed for it: the fireside chat. A few other talented, charismatic politicians of the 1930s similarly learned to use radio to establish a personal relationship with the voters. Mayor Fiorello LaGuardia of

New York read the comic strips to the public on New York City's own radio station, WNYC. Thus began a process which has grown into the spot television campaign of today.

The dual processes that we have just described of bureaucratization of social welfare and the emergence of personal political leadership via the electronic media have eroded party organizations steadily all through the last 35 years. Political clubs have grown fewer in number and smaller in attendance in this day of suburbia and electronic entertainment. The neighborhood club no longer serves the community functions that it once did, especially for urban ethnic areas. Precinct captains are largely a thing of the past. The street corner rally or torchlight parade is almost unknown in most campaigns. Clearly, politics have changed, but not as most commentators on the new politics would have us believe, in some dramatic way, in the last ten years. It is a change that has been taking place steadily and inexorably for over one-third of a century.

With the decline of the political party as an influence on the voter, the voter has become more independent. The evidence on this point is quite unambiguous. Table VIII-1 shows the percentage of voters who describe themselves as independents, as reported in various public opinion polls.

Table VIII-1. PARTY AFFILIATION OF VOTERS
BY OWN DECLARATION ON PUBLIC OPINION POLLS *

Year	Demo-cratic %	Republi-can %	Independ-ent %	Democratic % of two-party split
1940	42	38	20	$52\frac{1}{2}$
1950	45	33	22	58

(Continued)

Table VIII-1. (Cont'd.)

	Year	Demo-cratic %	Republi-can %	Independ-ent %	Democratic % of two-party split
	1960	47	30	23	61
	1964	53	25	22	68
June	1965	50	27	23	65
Oct.	1965	49	25	26	66
	1966	48	27	25	64
Feb.	1967	46	27	27	63
Oct.	1967	42	27	31	61
July	1968	46	27	27	63
July	1969	42	28	30	60
July-Aug.	1970	44	29	27	60

*Source, Gallup Opinion Index.

What we find is a rise since 1940 of about 7 percent in the number of independents, with about half of this increase occurring in a sudden jump in the latter half of 1965. It would be interesting to explore what combination of aftereffects of the 1964 landslide—the 1965 radical Great Society proposals and the heating up of the Vietnam War—led to some uprooting of political loyalties. For the moment the important fact is that it happened.

Table VIII-2 shows, for presidential years, the percentage of congressional districts in which the district voted for one party for President and for the other party for representatives in the House. In 1920 that was virtually an unknown phenomenon. The President's coattails carried congressmen with him. People tended to make a decision to vote for a party on election day; and whichever party they voted for, they tended to vote straight. By now, coattails no longer count for much. Malcolm Moos (1952, pp. 16-18) notes the same trend running from 1896, with the change dating to World War I. The trend has accelerated since then.

Table VIII-2.   PERCENT OF CONGRESSIONAL DISTRICTS
VOTING ONE PARTY FOR PRESIDENT
AND ANOTHER FOR HOUSE*

Year	%
1920	3.2
1924	8.7
1928	18.7
1932	12.8
1936	11.4
1940	13.3
1944	10.7
1948	17.3
1952	18.6
1956	29.2
1960	25.4
1964	33.3
1968	32.4

* 1920-1964 from cummings (1966). 1968 calculated from *Congressional Quarterly Almanac.* 1968 percentage omitting Wallace districts is still 25.6%.

In 1964 the large number of districts that split their vote could be attributed to the surge of the Johnson landslide which affected many normally Republican districts. In 1968, however, the election was close and quite normal. It was largely a replay of 1960. In both years the vote split 50-50 nationally; across states there was a correlation between the two elections of .90 in Nixon's percent of the total vote. Nonetheless split choices occurred in a third of all districts in 1968, in contrast to only one fourth of districts in 1960. The trend toward ticket-splitting is clear. How much ticket-splitting there is can be perceived if we realize that if random choices were operative in an evenly divided electorate, half the districts would by chance vote the same way for President and representatives and half would split. A third splitting instead of half shows some, but only a little, voter loyalty. True, that figure of a third counts a district as split if it went for Wallace for President and for a Democrat for the House (except in Alabama where Wallace got the Democratic label), but even without those Wallace districts the overall trend is clear. Increasingly the voters split their tickets, voting for the man—not the party.

Just about everything else that can be validly said about the new politics follows as a corollary from the decline of political parties. Voters still have to make up their minds. If party affiliation does not provide them with an easy answer as to how to vote, then some other guidelines must fill the vacuum. Thus, in a derivative way, it is true that issues, the candidate's personality, and the mass media all play a bigger role today than they did in the past, not because they have autonomously acquired a greater importance in the voter's life, but because a competing and dominant guideline has disappeared. These other elements have moved in to fill the vacuum. If a voter is willing to vote for either candidate, regardless of his party, then what the candidate says about Civil Rights, or whether he has a nice smile, or whether he has become familiar through frequent TV exposures, may all make a difference.

The role of issues, personality, mass media, and all such factors become more conspicuous in presidential years. In presidential elections the magnitude of the campaign means that by the end of it most voters have some fairly substantial image of each candidate. The tens of millions of dollars spent provide the voter with a reasonably filled-out notion of where candidates stand on the issues as reported in the media. With voters ready to swing between parties, the particulars of a campaign and of the candidates in it may cause rather massive movements in the electorate. Over the years the total presidential vote has split rather evenly. The mean two-party vote from 1932 through 1968 has been 53.1 percent Democratic and 46.9 percent Republican, and since World War II it has been 50.0 percent Democratic and 50.0 percent Republican. But while over the years the electorate has divided fairly evenly, the range has been between 42.2 percent Democratic in 1956 and 62.5 percent Democratic in 1936. These are percentages of the major party vote. It was not a long-run trend that accounted for the difference between the extremes of the range. That is indicated by the quick swing between 1956 and 1964, when the vote was 61.3 percent Democratic.

In other words, the vote can go 60-40 either way. Since in any one election people are switching in both directions, that means that many more than 10 percent of the voters shift when the vote goes from 60-40 one way to 60-40 the other.

Table VIII-3. DEMOCRATIC PERCENT OF THE
TWO-PARTY VOTE

	Number of elections	Average percent	Mean deviation
Presidential			
1948-1968	6	50.0	4.6
1932-1968	10	53.1	4.9
Congressional			
1946-1968	12	52.1	2.3
1932-1968	19	52.7	2.6

In congressional voting, the tides between elections swing somewhat less widely than they do between presidential elections. Over the same period of time, from 1932 through 1968, the extremes of congressional voting were in 1946, 45.3 percent Democratic, and in 1936, 58.5 percent Democratic, a range of 13.2 percentage points, as contrasted to a range of 20.3 percentage points for presidential elections. The mean deviation from the 10-election average of the two-party presidential vote has been 4.9 percentage points since 1932. For House elections the mean deviation has been 2.6 points or about half. (See Table VIII-3.)

Two theories account for the narrow swing between congressional elections. One hypothesis is that such special factors as candidate personality, issues, and media impact play a relatively minor role in the average congressional contest because most voters pay so little attention to it that they do not even know the name of their congressman. For that reason many voters on election day, lacking other cues, fall back on their conventional party preference. The other theory is that when the special factors of candidates, issues, and media do operate, they operate differently in different districts and tend to cancel each other out, leaving the net congressional vote nationally more nearly representative of normal party affiliations than in presidential voting. A glance at studies of single constituencies suggests that the second is the more powerful explanation (Moos, 1952, Chap. 4). In individual constituencies there is sometimes more and sometimes less variation in congressional than in presidential voting. Nationally, however, congressional voting is clearly more stable.

If these facts were better understood, there would have been a lot less wild speculation in the media about the recent congressional elections of 1970. We do not yet have official returns permitting analysis to three decimal places. Apparently, however, the Democratic party received its expectable

261

52 percent of the vote, exactly its normal vote. With that they gained a few (specifically nine) seats. That is what the most reasonable prediction would have been from the fact that in the previous (1968) congressional election they received 50.9 percent of the vote. In short, closing one's eyes to all the political facts of 1970—to the Vietnam War, to the trend in prices and employment, to the issue of law and order—but only assuming that whatever deviation there had been last time, the most likely change was a return to normalcy (or as it is technically called in the jargon, regression to the mean), would have led to a correct prediction of the outcome.

It is this regression to the normal party vote in off years that largely accounts for the so-called off year pendulum. The fact that the party holding the White House has gained seats in off years only once in this century is widely interpreted as an off year pendulum explainable by a disenchantment of the electorate with the party in power. There is something to that. But the swing is not mainly in off years; it is mainly in the presidential years. In estimating what will happen in an off year like 1970, one should look not so much at the year itself as at what happened the last time. If in 1968 the Republican party had come into power with a smashing victory, they would have held more seats and therefore would have lost in 1970. As it was, Nixon won the White House by a narrow streak, while the Democrats came in first in the congressional voting with 50.9 percent of the votes, a relatively small deviation from their average. Therefore one should have expected only a small change in the following off year, 1970.

The 1970 election fit that model. It confirms our belief that the American political system is rather persistent and unchanging. Such an analysis of the past, however, should not be confused with an absolute prediction. There were many wild predictions floating around before the 1970 election: predictions of a vast conservative surge, of a revolt of the electorate against the war in Vietnam, of an electorate ready to kick over the traces, of a new Republican majority based on a swing of the blue-collar voters. These predictions were all wrong, but they were not inconceivable. If any of these things had been happening, then now, in retrospect, we would be looking at a congressional vote departing from the 52-48 division that is normal. There have been such off years with swings as wide as 6 percentage points away from the average, and these did indicate genuine voter concern about something and potential reorientation on the part of the electorate. In 1946 the electorate was expressing a basic war-weariness, an anxiety about the future, and a tedium with years of crisis and sacrifice. In 1964 the voters were expressing a genuine alarm at the implications of Republican conservatism and nuclear irresponsibility. But in the absence of even a 3 or 4 percent drift of the vote away from its normal party division in 1970, there is really nothing to explain. Inflation, the war in Vietnam, the crises on the campuses are all there, but they explain nothing. 1970 was the most normal of possible years. Indeed that is the fact that needs to be explained. Why were the voters so little moved by a series of issues that our press and our alarmist intellectuals believe have moved this country to the verge of panic and dismay?

There is no simple answer to the voters stolidity. The explanation is in part that the problems are not as bad as the alarmists would have us believe, and in part that neither party has a monopoly on the cures. Unemployment and inflation are serious, but in our highly buffered economy major suffering from them is still more often a threat than a reality. The war in Vietnam is serious, but violence is being systematically reduced, and so is the size of the American commitment. Crime on the streets is serious, as is the decay of that part of the younger generation that has embraced the escapisms of revolution and drugs; but in hard quantitative terms these things are not increasing nearly as much as popular mythology would have us believe. Nonetheless, whatever the realities, the public is concerned. But concern alone is not enough to change votes. Before votes change, one must believe that the candidates or parties make a difference on these issues.

On most current issues the two parties have blurred images. On economic issues, the differences between the administration and its critics have become highly technical and subtle. We are all Keynsians these days. It is only a matter of timing and degree. On Vietnam it is hard to believe that any American administration of either party would act very differently. Vietnamization had started under the previous administration; and it is inconceivable that any Democrat who might have replaced Johnson, or might replace Nixon in the future, would do other than to try to wind down the war. He might do it a little more or a little less than Nixon is doing, but that is all. Above all, crime in the streets is not something about which either party, regardless of its claims, knows what to do.

The members of the electorate were fairly rational in 1970 in not seeing any issue or issues that pushed them sharply away from the basic positions and alignments that each of them had as individuals. The Republicans could easily vote Republican, and the Democrats could dissent enough from current realities to vote Democratic, and neither needed to feel much conflict about it.

What does this foretell for 1972? Both parties have reason for optimism and hope. Nixon is not whistling in the dark, as many Democrats would like to believe, in expressing satisfaction with the results of the 1970 elections. He belongs to, and presumably knows that he belongs to, the minority party. But he also knows that the Democratic percentage of the electorate, according to poll identifications, has fallen from 68 to 60 percent of the two-party total since 1964 (cf. Table VIII-1). He knows, further, that he has certain advantages as the incumbent and as the candidate of the party with more money and better technical expertise in campaign management. He knows also that the Republicans have systematically turned out their vote better than the Democrats. That is why an electorate divided 60-40, Democrats vs. Republicans, votes 52-48 in congressional elections and 50-50 in presidential elections. Balancing all these considerations, he has an altogether reasonable chance of coming through, not with a landslide that will represent a shift in the basic character of American politics but with another narrow victory. In the absence of major reasons to the contrary, the closely divided American electorate is not likely to throw out the incumbent.

On the other hand, the Democrats certainly have a chance. They are, and remain, the majority party. Discontent is widespread in the land. This administration has shown little talent for popular mobilization or for creation of enthusiasm. A well-organized Democratic campaign, with an attractive candidate, would have the usual campaign effect of drawing people back to their normal party alignment and could bring the White House back into Democratic hands.

There is no reason now in 1970 to predict any changes in 1972 more dramatic than those. 1972 is likely to be a reasonably close, hard-fought election, not yet foreseeable as to outcome. It always remains possible that exogenous events will cause a major shift in the electorate. Such exogenous events, if they occur, are most likely to take place in the outside world rather than in the domestic arena; war in the Middle East, a Communist takeover in Vietnam, war anywhere involving American troops, or for that matter, Communist takeovers anywhere following on American inactivity could have a profound effect. So could serious depression or booming prosperity, but the former is hardly likely in this day and age.

I am not trying to provide a crystal ball. All these speculations are relevant only insofar as they bear upon our subject, the new politics. What I am saying in effect is that there is not a great deal that is so very new. Barring extreme events, the pattern of 1970—and likewise the pattern of 1972—is, and can be expected to be, reasonably close to the pattern of American politics for several decades in the past. All that is new is that, the hold of party having weakened, the electorate has somewhat more potential for volatile changes if one party or the other acquires a distinct advantage in either the attractiveness of its candidates, the balance on some current issue or issues, or its media skills and media budget. These things in most instances will cancel out, leaving the election results roughly in line with party divisions, but they can no longer be dismissed to the degree that they could have been dismissed 40 years ago on the assumption that in the end party would win out over all.

It is perhaps not particularly fruitful to speculate at this point as to whether one or the other party will in the future have a distinctly more attractive candidate. It is somewhat more fruitful to speculate as to whether emerging issues are likely to give one party or the other a distinct issue advantage. My guess about that would be that the chances for a realignment resulting from issues is rather small in the short run, though perhaps considerable in the long run. In the short run, the similarity between the two parties and the broad base of each of them make issue differentiation unlikely. There is no critical current issue, such as federal social welfare activities in the 1930s or the tariff earlier, that could act as a touchstone to party alignment. Nor is there any major sector of the American public that dissents very drastically from the middle-of-the-road policies of the two parties on the major current issues. We on the campuses of the Northeast are overly conscious of the radical dissent against the war and of the kind of rejection of present society that the current faddist formulation is calling a third consciousness. In the short run, however, there are not many votes to be had on those issues, as Scammon, Wattenburg, and others have so effectively pointed out. The educated young, in which this dissent is concentrated, are not the heart of the electorate.

But let us not engage in a putdown. Those who comfort themselves by the fact that more of the electorate is put off by the radical young than is mobilized by them may well be riding for a surprise and a fall. The fact of the matter is that the ideas of the future are likely to be the ideas of the educated, youthful elite of today.

Between 17 and 22 most people adopt political views that tend to stick with them for a lifetime, moderated perhaps, but usually not drastically changed, thereafter. Critical elections and the traumatic social events that produce them (such as depressions, revolutions, mass movements, and wars) do convert some mature adults, but to an even greater degree they shape the generation who are young adults when they occur.

Such a period of traumatic events and massive conversions has some effect on electoral results at once but also a larger delayed effect as the 17 to 22-year-olds fully join the electorate. It is well established that nonvoting is high in very young cohorts. In seven or eight years, however, they will have largely joined the voting population. The electoral impact of critical events is thus partly delayed. So after a critical election, for a few years the winner in the new realignment will continue to gain strength as the conservative, older cohorts die off and the most changed, younger cohorts become voters.

That is just the first wave of effects of a critical election. A generation later, a second wave may come, as children inherit their parents' politics. It has been frequently noted, for example, that the radical college students of 1968-1969 are children of radicals of an earlier generation (Keniston, 1968). A major trauma in the years of political socialization of a cohort will show up to some degree in the generation of its children.

Consider the cohort whose political socialization was molded in 1932. We may call that the cohort of the early New Deal, traumatized by the depression and the great reform plans of the CCC, NRA, AAA, WPA, etc. These men of 17 to 22 in 1932 were Kennedy's New Frontiersmen, aged 45 to 50 in 1960; their children of 17 to 22 in 1960 responded in the second wave to the Kennedy charisma. (The median difference in age of father and child is 29 years; mother and child, 26.)

Another overlapping cohort we shall call the late or radical New Deal. (Generations, of course overlap; there are no breaks in the stream of time.) That generation who were 17 to 22 in 1935, 1936, or 1937 had their traumas in the sit-in strikes of the CIO, the Spanish Civil War, and the struggle against the rising cloud of war and fascism. Twenty-eight years after 1936, in 1964, the Great Society having won a landslide election, their children proceeded to enact health, civil rights, urban, and education bills that expressed the frustrated demands of the thirties. What had been too radical then was now accepted.

An overlapping cohort was the generation whose political trauma was World War II. The younger ones of them, those 17 to 22 by 1940 were still partly shaped by the depression, the New Deal, and the isolationist, keep-out-of-war sentiments of before Pearl Harbor. The older ones of them who did not reach draft age until 1943 or 1944 felt only the war, not the early radicalizing political experience. Both of these cohorts, in contrast to the previous ones, underwent the massive brutalization and alienation of war, but the more so the later they came into political maturity, and the less they had of prewar political experience. Their children are the alienated young of today. The parents of the McCarthy kids of 1968 were on the average socialized politically in 1940. By 1970 the youth movement was showing antimilitarism and a propensity for violence, cynicism, and alienation unprecedented in this country. The grim seeds of war were bearing fruit in the children of the World War II generation.

What I have been outlining is the merest sketch of an

hypothesis. It is far from a well-tested theory. One way in which it may be tested is by prediction. It has implications for prediction for 1972 and after. The impressionable young for the next few years are the second wave of the later, post-New Deal, GI generation, those whose socialization occurred between 1942 and 1945. Following on them comes a wave, about ten years long, of children of the private, quite conservative, anti-Communist, antipolitical, (Joe) McCarthy-scared generations of the postwar years.

All of this suggests conservatism as the youth trend for the immediate future, moderated in the electorate by the fact that the new and slightly radicalized youth of 1960 to 1968 will increasingly be part of the voting population for the next few years. At the same time, there is good reason to expect that in the later 1980s there will be a new wave of popular support for radical reform. But it would be taking a model far too seriously to treat that as a firm prediction now. If we leave the dates aside, however, I would with some confidence predict that after a period of some seeming quiet and retardation of change, there will come a renewed and successful surge of radical ideology partially incorporating some of the extreme ideas of the radical college youth of today. Though they might dislike the idea, the fact of the matter is that these Ivy League dissidents are the emerging establishment. They are the candidates for the key opinion-forming jobs. The ideas to which this generation is socialized are the ideas that they will carry with them for the rest of their lives, perhaps in drastically modified, but still recognizable, form. Their alienation, their disenchantment, their sentimental, ideological, rather than practically self-interested, approach to politics will not vanish even if the topics addressed do change. We have not seen the end of the ideas of the New Left. The consequences of these ideas will be partially incorporated into the standard thinking of the American establishment, perhaps in the 1980s and 1990s. My soberest prediction would be conservative politics for the immediate future with the Republicans doing reasonably well electorally, and with the Democrats moving to the right. The public is turning against the militants of 1969. But beyond 1972 and beyond the usual horizon of our political thinking, there is reason to expect a sharp resurgence of the antiauthoritarian, antimilitarist, equalitarian, antiorganizational, and hedonistic values of the contemporary Left into the mainstream of American politics.

Contemporaneously with that will also come a decomposition of the mass audience, as channels for electronic communication multiply. This may either force a revival of effective political party organization as the means for managing the new complex of communication channels; or, if that does not happen, it will cause a great increase in depolitization. If the latter is what occurs, coupled with the entry into seats of power by the college generation of today, then, at some point 20 or more years hence, there may come about the kind of reconstruction of American politics that is often erroneously described as the new politics of today: alienated, sentimental, unconventional, disenchanted, and dominated not by the party "pols" but by alumni of academia working as managers of the game of politics. That has not occurred yet, and it will not occur soon. Indeed, if the parties respond effectively to the challenge of proliferating communication channels and provide a means for orchestrating their diversity, then it may never occur.

REFERENCES

Berelson, Bernard, Lazarsfeld, Paul F., and McPhee, William, *Voting*, Chicago: U. of Chicago Press, 1954.

Burnham, Walter Dean, *Critical Elections and the Future of American Politics*, New York: W. W. Norton, 1970.

Campbell, Angus, Converse, Philip E., Miller, Warren, and Stokes, Donald, *The American Voter*, New York: Wiley, 1960.

Converse, Philip, E., "Electoral Change in the United States," in *The Human Meaning of Social Change*, Angus Campbell and Philip E. Converse, eds., New York: Russell Sage Foundation, forthcoming.

Converse, Philip E., Miller, Warren E., Rusk, Jerrold G., and Wolfe, Arthur C., "Continuity and Change in American Politics: Parties and Issues in the 1968 Election," *American Political Science Review*, Vol. LXIII (Dec. 1969), No. 4, pp. 1083-1105.

Cummings, Milton C., Jr., *Congressmen and the Electorate: Elections for the House and the President, 1920-1964*, New York: The Free Press, 1966.

Janowitz, Morris, Wright, Deil, and Delany, William, *Public Administration and the Public Perspectives Toward Government in a Metropolitan Community*, Ann Arbor: U. of Michigan, Bureau of Government, Institute of Public Administration, Michigan Governmental Studies, No. 36, 1958.

Keniston, Kenneth, *Young Radicals*, New York: Harcourt Brace, 1968.

Lang, Kurt and Lang, Gladys, *Politics and Television*, Chicago: Quadrangle Press, 1968.

Lazersfeld, Paul F., Berelson, Bernard, and Gaudet, Hazel, *The People's Choice*, New York: Columbia U. Press, 1944.

Moos, Malcolm, *Politics, Presidents, and Coattails*, Baltimore: The Johns Hopkins Press, 1952.

Pool, Ithiel de Sola, "TV: A New Dimension in Politics," in Eugene Burdick and Arthur Brodbeck, eds., *American Voting Behavior*, Glencoe, Ill.: The Free Press, 1959.

Reiss, Albert J., *Occupations and Social Status*, New York: The Free Press, 1961.

Rosenbloom, David, *Managers in Politics*, Ph.D., thesis, Dept. of Political Science, M.I.T., Cambridge, Mass. 1970.

Alienation, Protest, and Rootless Politics in the Seventies

by Robert E. Lane
Professor of Political Science,
Yale University, and *President,*
American Political Science Association

The closing days of a year ending in zero occasionally have the unfortunate effect of stimulating a set of anxious men to speak about the decade ahead, a practice with unknown consequences but not entirely harmless. Trespassing on 1971 I take this opportunity to join this group, dealing in this special case with some observations on alienation, protest politics, and the emerging problems of a kind of unanchored or "rootless politics." It will be clear from the futuristic cast of these comments, as well as from the nature of the topics, that the observations are speculative in nature and on the extreme soft end of the hardness-softness scale employed by so many social scientists to designate the reliability of observations if not the moral character of the observer.

I employ the term alienation here to mean the rejection of the dominant values, social norms, and conventions of a society or that portion of society in which a person lives, or at least the portion that he notices. The alienated may take alternative courses of action. One of these is to withdraw into isolation, where he may live in a kind of curdled milieu of unhappiness and malaise or may try to reconstruct a mini-life with something called a life style more congenial to an alternative set of norms, values, and conventions representing a form of counter culture. The other course is to protest the norms that are so offensive and either anomically to strike out against them or, alternatively, to organize a set of protests and efforts at restructuring things to make the larger society more congenial. First I will speak generally about alienation without differentiating between these two (withdrawal vs. protest) means of adjusting to it; then I will turn to the protest syndromes of the near—that is, ten-year—future.

To understand the future of alienation it is essential that we first come to understand one of its major sources, setting aside (begging, if you like) the question of whether the world is not really so hideously offensive that only the sane are alienated. This major source, I believe, is the social denigration of certain sets of persons who experience their environment as threatening to their self-esteem, who feel that their rightful place in the world as they see it is jeopardized, whose sense of prideful belonging is threatened, who say in effect to their unfriendly environment, "You have hurt me; I will have none of your ways." Naturally, under such circumstances, the threatened or denigrated individual will discover a set of alternative values which restore his sense of self-esteem and belonging and have the virtue of putting down the society that seems to him to be putting him down.

If we have correctly located one of the major sources of alienation, it follows that we can make some pretty good guesses about who will be alienated both in general and in more specific terms. Generally speaking marginal men at the intersection of two cultures or subsocieties will find themselves threatened, with their persons judged by competing standards and their sense of belonging undermined. Traditionally we have thought of these as ethnic assimilators, the socially mobile (especially downward mobile), and adolescents. Perhaps more accurately one could designate the likely victims of alienation as those whose social functions are threatened: the technologically obsolescent (card-index librarians confronted with computerized information retrieval); the performers of an art left behind in a wave of changing fashion (fiction writers in an age of nonfiction); or, along similar lines, failing elites, either establishment or revolutionary (WASP editors of the failing media, former Communists). The reader will grasp the common theme: wherever society catches a person in a conflict where what he knows and what he is seem undervalued, the temptations of alienation are great.

In one sense the great society is almost always ambiguous about how it values an individual, thus inviting alienation to an unprecedented degree. Further, it should be noted that alienation is greatly assisted by the invention of the term "alienation" and the development of a literature as well as the discussion of the phenomenon in the media. Without these aids to self-understanding, a person might just feel unhappy, lacking the label that packages his unhappiness and gives it back to him as a recognizable syndrome.

Specifically, then, we would expect the following kinds of people to be alienated:

1. Artists of the high culture in a world so appreciative of kitsch. It is little wonder that they feel unappreciated (because they are) and little wonder that the apparatus of alienation is so attractive.

2. Humanists challenged by the social scientists and by the organization men *(Le Defi Americaine)*, substantive philosophers challenged by methodological philosophers (who may tell them their world views rest on semantic confusions), teachers of language challenged by linguistics (who talk a strange language of information theory), psychoanalysts challenged by empirical psychology, and so forth. When a domain of knowledge becomes scientized, not always to its benefit, there is much resentment among the members of the residual group, a resentment that finds expression in alienation and a satisfaction in the inevitable pratfalls of the new pretenders to the ancient crown.

3. Students threatened by each other, by the "high standards" of the established elites, especially in an age when "excellence" becomes the catchword of the teaching profession. Fearful lest they do not have enough of this "excellence" and uncertain of how to achieve it—because they do not see so much of it exemplified in their models and mentors— therefore worried about themselves and their standing among these standards, they find the alienation mystique felicitous and rewarding.

4. The working poor, having achieved some respectability at the cost of hard work and impulse denial, who see these

virtues set at naught by what they regard as the easy access to relief of the unscrupulous, or the political purchase of benefits by the protesting minorities. The alienation here takes the form of disenchantment with the welfare state they once espoused and with the elites that foster a something-for-nothing ethos, making their own achievements and therefore themselves worthless.

5. Intellectuals who feel themselves unappreciated in a mass society, where demcoracy counts them as only one man with only one vote and where, for all their culture and learning, they are called "Pop" by the garage man and "Mac" by the friendly policeman. The deference deficit they experience is a continuing problem as they seek to balance their precarious ego books at the end of the day.

Alienation, like other phenomena, develops counter forces, and the counter-alienation forces can be more destructive than their targets. They take the form, of course, of denigration of the critics, glorification of the traditional, reverence of the familiar, hostility towards the questioners, nostalgia, piety, and a language clotted with such phrases as "fouling their own nests," "the culture of failure," and "go back where you came from." If a root cause of alienation is threat to self-esteem and place, one root of the malevolence toward the alienation is the tenuousness of a man's grasp on his own professed values. Aesthetically, the alienated are not a pretty lot, but that is no reason for malevolence. Rather we must seek for the sources of the malevolent impulse in the very attractiveness of the forbidden alienation themes. The reasoning here is familiar: those wishes or impulses that we have just barely repressed or controlled are the most dangerous ones, hence they require the strongest charge of emotion to oppose. In this opposition, the friendly help of one's own anger, contempt, and hatred is a valuable asset, for among other things, the expressions of these emotions help to reassure the vulnerable square that he does not secretly admire the illicit alienation pathologies. For these reasons, we find the malevolent counter-alienation forces to be the psychological neighbors of those alienated themselves but rutted too deep in routine to escape, bonded to conventions they dare not challenge.

It would be a mistake, however, to believe that the explanation of malevolent counter-alienation rests entirely on the tenuousness of repression and control, for fear of confusion and the dislike of the unfamiliar are also powerful motives. The very thing that makes a person a fundamentalist in religion (if he has any choice) and a patriot in his self-identification makes him hostile to alienation. He chooses these patterns (or absorbs them into his self-system) because of their reassuring absoluteness. To rethink the matter is doubly distasteful for it implies that the world he knows might be wrong, or, worse, that he might be wrong. Further, rethinking anything in a world with a crowded agenda of career-relevant worries is troublesome. Faced by these considerations, clearly the counter-alienation forces have a store of reasons for investing some emotion in hating the alienated. There are, of course, other good reasons for counter-alienation, some of them having to do with investments in friendships, property, and rationales for one's own achievements, as well as powerful forces of psychic inertia. It is enough to know that the counter-alienation forces have their tanks full of adrenalin, bile, and vinegar for such trips as need to be fueled on short notice.

The media foster and inhibit alienation in several conflicting ways. If alienation develops where men feel their self-esteem and their sense of belonging threatened, we should look to the media for such threats. First, perhaps, is the constant replay of the success theme, the glory in celebrity, the "making it" posture, the attention to the great stage that makes life's little everyday stages seem so unimportant. In a community, one can measure himself by his neighbor. In a living room fifteen years ago, one could measure himself against his friends; now in that living room, the television set is turned on and the measures change. The dailyness of life is demeaned. The alienated strike back against the glittering tawdry world that does this to him.

How can a man individualize himself when the message bearers are massified? A book is individual; I am reading it alone. A diet of books is infinitely individualized, contributing to the sense of personal growth and enhancing the capacity for idiosyncratic conversation. If there is a drive towards self-actualization, as Maslow and Allport have argued,[1] surely the multiple pattern-cutting machines of the media frustrate that drive. If, as we shall argue, one of the virtues of the media is that everyone can discuss the same things with similar knowledge bases, the great vice of the media is that everyone says the same thing.

But there is another argument that emerges from some of the sensory deprivation literature, as I have just learned from an unpublished paper by Ronald Libby.[2] While sensory deprivation seems the last thing one would expect from the media, some of the sensory deprivation experiments reveal that it is the deprivation of *meaningful* stimulation that creates the pathologies associated with sensory deprivation;

noise and repetitious stimulation are also dangerous. Since, as Libby points out, one of the characteristics of the alienated described by Keniston is a thirst for alternative experiences that are somehow meaningful, and this is also a characteristic of those who have had a deprivation of meaningful stimulie in the laboratory, it is possible to conclude that alienation and the deprivation of meaningful messages or stimuli have something in common. And, with something of a further inferential leap, one might hypothesize that the media, with their plethora of stimuli that are neither coherent nor meaningful to the elite members of their audiences, help produce alienated youth in these strata. The emphasis here should be on the incoherence, disjunctiveness, cacophonous quality of media stimulation, a point to which I return in a later discussion.

Protest Politics

Protesters may or may not be alienated; they may reject the dominant values of society and seek something close to total change, or they may accept these values—indeed embrace them—and seek through protests to restore them where they have been challenged. Oddly enough, as in the case of the hard hat attack on peace marchers or the old-fashioned White race riots against Negroes, the restoration protesters seem to attack nongovernmental objects, whereas the protesters against the dominant or traditional norms seem to attack governmental targets or their surrogates, like university administrations. Nevertheless, in current climates and circumstances the champions of protest politics are those who, while they may not be alienated, are discontented with the going order and the values that inform and guide it. Discontent plus aggression seem to characterize enough of the phenomena called protest politics (student sit-ins, peace marchers, Black disturbances, tenant strikes, etc.) to serve as the touchstones of this discussion.

The media are not innocent of influence in this arena, but their effects run in several different directions and emerge from different features of their presentations. There are four theories of media influence that deserve our attention. The first is the *pacification theory*, if one may use a word currently in disrepute. This theory holds that there can be no important social protest in a world where much of society is glued to a cathode tube or, to change the metaphor, where narcosis and narcissus make common cause. The explanation does not rest so much on the dampening of the impulse to protest as it does on the creation and channeling of attitudes and energies by certain frequent television themes. Among these are that consumption is the purpose of life, that life is properly lived vicariously, and that the dominant values not only come through the ether but belong to the heavenly order of things. Alternatively, it might be argued that the bright world of television presents living evidence that opportunity lies everywhere, and that only the individual's failure to bestir himself can account for his failure to join the beautiful people.

Clearly, if the first generation of tube babies is also the protest generation, there is something wrong with the power of the pacification theory to explain current events.

The second theory of media influence on the propensity to protest (and to reject the dominant values of society) is the *cynicism theory*. Holders of this view argue that the dissonance between reality and the entertainment and commercialized world of television can only be reduced by a firm posture of disbelief and a resolution not to be taken in. The tube is the city slicker, the secondhand car salesman, the come-on artist. The world of television is a plastic, make-believe world. The rhetoric of television is deceitful; its style is hyperbole; its message is "watch-out." If the entertainment and commercial order is filled with fantasy, the news is filled with comfortless reports of trouble, at variance with the residues of the American dream learned in school. Both entertainment and news pose the question: "What should I believe?" With plural voices offering various suggestions, the question becomes: "Whom should I believe?" To these questions the media offer no answers; and it is, so the theory goes, only prudent for the bewildered individual to answer "nothing" and "nobody."

If, on top of these ragged difficulties, a viewer finds himself barbed by the "many tiny messages" of the media, overstimulated by the inconsequential, he may find blessed relief in turning off his mind while letting his senses do the best they can with the pin-pricking waves of sound and light. In either case, so the theory goes, the audioviewer withdraws into a kind of disbelief where the temptations to protest are unlikely to find him.

Those who hold this view tend to argue that it is wise to allow politics into the media only where there is a strong commercial element, for it is the habitual discounting of media messages, learned from experience with advertising and commerce, that teaches an appropriate skepticism toward politics.

The *disorientation theory* is not incompatible with the cynicism theory, but it purports to explain public confusion not public skepticism. Where the cynicism theory holds that television and to a lesser extent the daily press lead people to disbelieve public messages, putting together a world view of events as improbabilities and meanings as inscrutable, the disorientation theory holds that people are more likely to adopt bits and pieces of what they see and hear, putting them together in eclectic and personalized confusion. The argument rests on two features of media presentation: (1) the fragmentation of news dissociated from coherent interpretation; and (2) the inchoate emotionalism of the media, the sensation salad on its bill of fare.

Inevitably the presentation of news as it happens will make the patterns underlying events obscure; contemporaneity is not a satisfactory organizing principle for understanding causes or for constructing patterns. Without a theory events don't make sense; thus a person is tempted to impose upon them some simple homemade explanatory rubrics, such as a conspiracy theory where "they" stands for the complex agencies that govern or seem to govern the world. If not that, there are available some simplistic doctrines of exploitation, whether by class or race, that may help in aggregating the fragments of the news, provide motives and causes, and give the illusion of understanding. It takes some effort to employ even such explanations, however, and for the most part it is not worth it because there is no perceived gain; hence the fragments are allowed to cumulate in the mind like shards of broken glass at the bottom of the wastebasket.

The alternative, I suppose, is to provide a steady exposure to events as interpreted by a more or less coherent—that is, ideological—world view and framed by premises that are all compatible with one another, or vague enough to give that illusion. Failing this, the individual could himself be indoctrinated by a ready-made ideology into which he can fit news items. Both are repulsive and improbable, given the looseness and incompleteness of Marx, market theory, Talcott Parsons, and cybernetics.

While these matters deal with the question "What should I believe?", the related question, "What should I feel?" finds no more satisfactory answers in the media offerings. No doubt the basic emotional tropisms are laid down early: despair, hope, a prudential constriction of emotion to the here and now, empathy, sympathy, apathy towards others. They all have childish origins, perhaps genetic ones. But the media arouse and evoke emotions, perhaps to some extent they pattern sets of emotional responses, they may bind (in the Freudian sense) emotions looking for objects, they channel and obstruct emotional responses. To the extent that commercial statements "use up" available emotions, they prevent an orderly flow into public affairs; hysterical advertising trivializes good emotional words and erodes their powers to evoke. The disjuncture between the sober presentation of a tragic mass drowning in Pakistan, the horror of Mylai, and the bright elation over a new soap ingredient for home use, wrenches the emotions. Without evidence, I would guess that such confabulations of mood-laden events lead to shallow emotions, impede the mobilization of emotions appropriate to the occasion, and legitimize that tendency that is present in all of us: the elevation of the personal trivia (the irritation of a hangnail) over the significant and enduring issues that affect self and others (the pathos of the cities, Black rage, death and destruction in Vietnam). The media orient and disorient; like a neurosis, they may promote for their readers and viewers a strategy of secondary gain, the gain of the short-term and immediate objectives at the cost of enduring, primary, life-long satisfactions.

While the cynicism and disorientation theories seem to promote inner conflicts of a certain kind, they may reduce social conflict by privatizing social problems or inhibiting conflict responses. But since the media deal directly with social conflict, no doubt there are more direct influences at work; and it is these that I wish briefly to examine under the fourth heading of the theories here under review, the *channeling of social conflict*. On the one hand, the mere reporting of abuses of power, the exploitation of men, the unredressed grievances of the disadvantaged, the absurdity of conventional arrangements stimulate protest. The report itself is a form of protest, and an effective one, for some policy-makers take as their assignment the reordering of things to reduce absurdity and to reform abuse. Further, it is probably true that the street protest, the sit-in by welfare mothers, the petition by disturbed professors are important because they are considered as news by the media reporters and editors. This makes them news and that makes them effective (if they are effective at all).

But there are major features of media structure and behavior that tend to reduce social conflict and inhibit its expression. One of these is the unsegregated audiences of any single newspaper or broadcasting station. The monopoly of the press in the one-paper city and the unselectivity of the airwaves promote an exposure to the same sets of materials by Catholics, Protestants, and Jews, by Blacks and Whites, by businessmen and their employees, by young and old. An alternative pattern would be, as in some countries, a Catholic press and a Protestant press, a working-class newspaper and broadcasting station owned by the unions, and a middle-class paper or network owned and operated by and for the bourgeoisie, and so forth. While these segregated media and segregated audiences and segregated appeals may serve some interests better some of the time, the advantage of unsegregated media and appeals lies in the introduction, if nothing more, of each group to the thought, heroes, and problems of the others. Perhaps this all works to favor the dominant White middle class by muting dangerous issues; perhaps it also helps to move majorities towards social change in slower but more consensual patterns. However it is appraised, the lack of segregated audiences tends to reduce conflict in the American society.

Television does more than introduce each side of a conflict to the problems and needs of the other side; it presents a spokesman of the other side to an audience in a form of human portraiture that tends to take the evil out of him. Seen as men, the opposition leaders are less easily hated than when they are seen as symbols. It is easier to hate the evil words in print, for they do not reveal the common humanity of their author. To many liberals Spiro Agnew is the symbol of all that is wrong with the Republican Establishment; on television he evokes mixed emotions, where human and ideological cues become confounded.

The common viewing, listening, and reading patterns of a large portion of the public tend, I believe, to set for the nation some common foci of attention, some common agendas of discussion. A reference to an issue or to a presentation of an issue is likely, in most social sets, to meet with recognition because of the overlapping exposure patterns of the members of these sets. Of course, people have different private and group agendas and these make for varied arenas of discourse, but the tendency of the media to homogenize sets means the variation is reduced, and the national agenda develops a meaningful cross-set audience and dialogue. Does talking about the same things on the basis of some recognition of the arguments on the other side reduce conflict or merely aggregate grievances for larger conflict? The answer is not at all clear, but it is plausible to argue that conflict becomes most embittered when no action on any agenda is possible because people cannot agree on what should be taken up next. Stasis is the result, not the kind of incremental, if glacial, change that seems to characterize American society. If stasis is a more fertile source of alienation than slow change, slow change may be a more fertile source of protest politics. After all, not only is there something to protest about (the slowness of change) but a reason to believe protest is worthwhile (the possibility of change).

Alienation and Protest in the Seventies

For the mass of Americans there had been a decline of alienated sentiments for many years up until the mid-sixties. They had an increasing sense of control over their own destinies—an increasing sense that each was receiving his share of good luck, a decline in the yearning for some golden age when it was better to have been alive, an increase in the sense that politics was a legitimate and relatively clean enterprise. Further, there had been a gradual but marked increase in the willingness to accord honor and status and power to what had been out-groups: Catholics, Jews, Negroes, and, if the term "out-group" is allowed, women. The social distance between the rival partisan groups that alternate in power, the Democrats and the Republicans, declined in the fifties and sixties, leading both to a sense of the legitimacy of the opposition and to an increase in independence (the stakes in an opposition victory were not so great).[3] Then came the protests of the late sixties, the surfacing of a "counter-culture," the increasingly articulate rage of the Blacks at their persistent disadvantages, the revolt on the campus, and the emergence of new groups like welfare mothers and dissident priests with the presumption to petition for the redress of grievances. The great consensus seemed shattered.

We can anticipate that other voices will be heard, some strident and clamorous, some softer, speaking to the conscience of the inner ear. The lessons of protest politics cannot be unlearned, for the protesters have often received benefits along with scolding for their clamor. The scolding seems minor compared to the benefits; and one benefit, attention, is positively enhanced by the scolding. The Chicanos and the American Indians are surely gathering their forces for more formidable protests; teachers and ministers are just beginning to be heard from; the underemployed professionals currently have grievances that have not yet received organized attention, but they will; the rural poor are difficult to organize, but they will find a way as they did in the thirties. The institutionalized—patients, prisoners, soldiers—will no doubt increase their resistance to the constraints that surround them. If patrolmen, firemen, and sanitationmen can so dramatically improve their circumstances through collective bargaining, so can college professors. And if they can, some will.

On the one hand, one might say of this: it is merely an

extension of what has happened throughout American and Western history; the organization and public protest of the disadvantaged, with benefits to the protesters and no great cost to the general society, indeed with some positive benefits to society as all come nearer to fair shares of the social product. Or one might say we have entered into a period of intensified social conflict such that the fabric of society is threatened; the capacity to adapt to multiple demands so strongly pressed has now become impossible. In the same way that the inflationary settlements of wage demands in one industry can be absorbed by the economy if they do not serve as standards for all other industries, so the special treatment of one minority is only possible if other groups do not demand the same treatment. But this is to talk of stability and accommodation, not justice, for justice demands that the deprivations of history have to be recognized as posing claims that cannot be postponed.

If the morality of the situation is unclear, the prognosis, I believe, is a little less murky. Of the two interpretations of protest politics in the seventies, I prefer the more hopeful one. Protest politics, it seems to me, represent only a continuation of what we have known; the wave of protests do not constitute a threat to the fabric of society. The reasons have partly to do with the role of the media we have discussed: the media will pacify some, make some cynical and apathetic, disorient some, and stimulate the organization and activation of some. The media do not generally serve to mobilize the population for active protest. But there are other reasons for believing that we can live with, adapt to, and even benefit from the social protests of the seventies that go beyond the media and have their roots in current history and social organization.

The recent rise in protest politics has several sources. The first, having to do with the revolt of the students, is based on the belief that a large part of student disaffection with current society stems from the threat of conscription into the armed services for a war students and others have come to regard as immoral, foolish, wasteful, destructive. The sacrifice involved in armed service—the disruption of lives, careers, comfort, on-going purposeful existence—is enormous. The emotional charge thus generated directs attention to many allied grievances; it is freely available for other causes speaking the language of social justice; it is related to all facets of life, since conscription is total for a long period of time, and everything becomes potentially related to this particular grievance. It enlists aggression, sacrifice, and hostility; and because the young are brought together on college campuses, this emotional charge is commonly available to contiguous groups to facilitate their organization. It follows, therefore, that what is called "the winding down of the war" (if it really takes place) will greatly alter the emotional charges of the young and the sources of alienation and protest—not only for peace movements, but for many other movements which seem to have captured their minds and hearts. Moreover, since there is no social mechanism for one student generation to transmit a tradition to another, the momentum will quickly die, once the war is halted.

The revolt of the Blacks is another matter; for, as a more or less cohesive and continuing community with grievances beyond those of any other American group, the emotional charge behind the protests is not displaced but direct, the parent-child transmittal of a "revolutionary culture" is easy if not inevitable, the learned usefulness of protest is instructive to others, the leadership is continuous, the moral dimensions of the real grievances cause doubt and compromise in the White opposition and provide reinforcement for the protest movement, and the cross-group ties (ties between Blacks and Whites) are still so tenuous that there are few counter-pressures to mute the protest. Nevertheless, although the challenge is the greatest the nation has ever seen and the problem defies brief analysis, I believe the protest politics of the Blacks, and perhaps even their alienation, may change character in the seventies.

For one thing, the level of education has changed sufficiently to permit (sometimes under forced draft) the entrance of Blacks into the commercial, clerical, and even professional world. When this happens, class divisions, hence divisions on strategy, enter into the Black community. Further, to some minor extent, cross-race friendships or at least communications begin to open up under these circumstances; the totality of cultural separatism is eroded. Perhaps more important, that ingredient of the American culture that kept unionism from becoming socialist becomes operative: a member of the Black community may begin to sense that he can achieve many of his aims by individual, not group, effort. Further, party politics opens up opportunities, not only for better "balanced tickets," but for Black power in the great urban concentrations and in the rural Black communities. The possibilities for real power achieved through electoral processes reduce the pressure for protest politics.

If, as we have said, the effectiveness of protests depends upon media treatment, and if their lack of novelty makes protests increasinly less newsworthy, protests themselves lose their force. The protest organizations become bureaucratized as well as organized; their leaders have stakes in on-going bargaining relationships, patronage, small but real gains for members who may prefer these to the larger, if less certain, gains of disruptive protests. Protests become ritualized; charisma becomes routinized; protesting interests become vested.

Finally, society moves in two opposite directions to adjust to the new situation. On the one hand, it becomes repressive, changing the calculations of protesting groups. The stakes may become too high for the casual protester. On the other hand, it moves to institutionalize the handling of grievances: legal aid in ghettoes, class action suits, government enforcement of individual claims, and the establishment of ombudsmen or something like them in critical areas. Thus there are individual and group alternatives to protect politics. Finally, public and private agencies add Blacks to their committees, juries, boards; the grievances are learned at an earlier stage, and this intelligence is used both to frustrate protest and to remove grievances.

Those who come later in history, learning protest politics from the Blacks and students, now face a different set of circumstances. The protests are no longer new; the public is fatigued; the social order is better prepared. And, perhaps more important than anything else, what is familiar does not create a state of emergency or alarm. Much of the alarm over "the fabric of our society" was due to bewilderment over the apparent novelty of what was happening; now that we have seen what it is like, we know we can live with it, changing practices and institutions as may seem desirable or necessary. Braced, and more realistic about revolutionary rhetoric, many, including the protesters, will come down to earth where pragmatic bargains may be achieved. Protest and anti-protest states of minds can now deal with the familiar without the hysteria of the recent past.

The Problem of Rootless Politics

If the core of alienated politics is rejection and the core of protest politics is attack, the core of rootless politics is *flux*, the availability of fluid emotions and unattached loyalties for new political purposes. The concept of rootless politics is the result of four recent attitudinal, institutional, and legal developments. The first and probably the most important, both a consequence and a cause of rootlessness, is the declining strength of party identification. For about 12 years the number of people who think of themselves as independent of party and who split their ballots and switch their support from one election to the next has been growing. The second development, perhaps a cause of the first, is the transformation of the working class into the bourgeoisie, partly a matter of changing occupational structures and opportunities, partly a homogenization of life styles, partly the changed relationship between blue-collar wages and white-collar wages, partly, no doubt, a reflection of affluence, a reflection that may disappear under the stress of a prolonged recession.

The third development is the enfranchisement of younger voters, as a result of a slow movement in state law and, more importantly, of sudden congressional action. The eighteen, nineteen, and twenty-year olds have always been less committed to a particular party than older citizens; they have fewer economic "interests," fewer community roots of their own making, fewer political experiences to guide them. They are more available, more fluid. The fourth development is the reduction of a residence requirement, enfranchising a more mobile segment of the population and giving the vote to those who have not yet "settled" into their new communities.

These four developments have the common result of reducing the weight of tradition, personal and communal, in voting, and increasing the importance of current stimuli. In reducing the importance of party, class, and community cues, they increase the importance of other things, both internal and external. On the one hand, this new freedom gives scope to the political expression of a man's idiosyncratic personality; and on the other hand, it makes the media and other external cuing devices more important. Turning to these media influences, we may isolate a few of the consequences of media impact on rootless politics.

Lacking party and other cues that inform a voter how he should feel, vote, and think about a given issue, the voter seeks other guidance. The issues are complex; he rarely has the time to master them, hence he adopts the substitutes for explanation that are offered him: *slogans.* The first effect, then, is in part to sloganize elections; and here the media, with their spot advertising and "paid political announcements," offer just what the cueless voter needs. He finds such terms as "law and order," "permissiveness," "domino theory," and "communist aggression" to be persuasive. This is neither better nor worse than party cues; they are more personal and idiosyncratic, but they lack the mediating leadership of group spokemen that summarize or aggregate interests.

In addition to offering an excellent milieu of slogans, the media also offer an excellent means of *mood manipulation.* The press has its own ways of doing this (with headline and cartoon and imagery of many kinds), but television offers a more vivid and powerful instrument of mood instruction, as in the 1964 sequence where the little girl gives her version of a nuclear count down, counting petals to the point of a nuclear explosion. The media evoke predispositions towards "toughness" for the extra-punitive, of suspicion for the un-trusting, or faith and dependency for the gullible and passive. They may stress optimism or pessimism about the future, calling forth in men their latent sense that the future is open and promising, or that the future is dangerous, that one should habitually prepare for the worst, according to his own personal convictions. These are both powerful and dangerous, for lacking verbal content they are less available to consciousness, that is, to rational persuasion. If the cuing by party, class ties, or community sentiment lacks elements of rationality, at least the process suggests a chain of causes that links opinions to definable interests. The mood-cuing func-tions just described attenuate that reasoned, if loosely con-structed, linkage.

Much has been said of *candidate image-making* by men experienced in advertising and public relations, the packag-ing and selling of a congressman, governor, or president. Again television offers the greatest scope, for by selective presentation, building an image trait by trait, modeling a man for his "dynamism" his "fatherly countenance," his "plain folks" appeal, his "directness and candor," the media can give us the illusion of understanding a complex person-ality without the substance. Most people believe they are good judges of personality, something they have had some experience doing, even though they may believe they are poor judges of complex issues. The media can trade on this. Fortunately, the packaging of a personality is not so well understood as the packaging of a product; and the wise counsellors of Madison Avenue may be no more able to say what it is that will "sell" a given man, than a professor is able to say what it is that makes one man a good teacher and another one not. Nevertheless, the cuing of the image-makers is likely to produce a voting pattern different from that produced by the cuing of the party label, or established voting tradition, or the consensus of a community; it is more volatile, and it is less easily linked to enduring interests or to preferred policy consequences.

But this new "freedom of choice" offers the media another opportunity for influence, one that might improve the quality of choice and therefore the quality of politics. Platforms and programs do differ; candidates and their spokemen discussing these differences may be persuasive. *Reasoned argument* has a chance where party, class, and community cues are relaxed. The cuing function of these groups tends to deal with sets of people, with group interests; but individuals within these groups differ, and a man who listens to argument may, under the best circumstances, find individual positions that more nearly correspond with his individual needs, preferences, and interests.

One should not overstate the case for media influence; the skepticism we mentioned, borne of years of exposure to advertising, the competing claims of other group influences and loyalties, the strong personal traditions laid down early in childhood—all will limit media influences on voting decisions. But even if we are speaking of marginal influences, many elections, including presidential elections, are usually won by small margins. And in the American system victory and defeat are binary; for any one office a candidate either wins or he loses, however gross or slender his margin.

Rootless Politics and Governmental Policy

Whether or not the media "improve" electoral choices in the new era of rootless politics, the character of these choices will affect the operations of government and the policies that governments adopt. Traditionally, it has been the case that nonpartisan elections have tended to favor Republicans; for the Democrats, relying on working-class voters who need the party cue to guide them in situations where the press (and the bought time on television) are Republican, need an alternative guiding post. This may still be the case; the decline of party may seem to apply equally to all partisans, but the real implication is the decline of Democratic cues and the rise of Republican ones.

Even if this is not true, however, rootless politics have implications for the way governments function. For one thing, politics of this character both reflect and imply the further decline of the political machine, a device that required local party loyalty to operate effectively. Further, rootless politics imply a greater turnover in legislatures, for the year-in, year-out congressman or state legislator has relied heavily on his one-party constituency. He may, of course, be able to persuade his constituents anew at each election, but he must face greater risks where the party loyalty that has kept him in office begins to erode. The new face and new appeal that may emerge at any election now have a better chance of converting his party-free constituents.

This possibility of more rapid turnover among legislators and executives has further implications. One of them is loss of experience in office; the seasoned expert who has mastered a field (agriculture, taxes, transportation) during his years of tenure may go down before the fresh new personality. The compensating gain, of course, is the fresh new point of view that this personality brings with him. Policies need reexamination; the government of rootless politics may provide more of this.

No doubt the legislatures will lose more power than the executives in the fluidity that rootless politics implies, for legislatures require the organizing principles of party in order to be effective. As voters lose their party consciousness, so also will legislators; and hence legislatures may fragment into a variety of issue-oriented clusters, changing as the issues change. Such coalitions must, however, be unstable without party cement to give them continuity, a continuing leadership, and an organized basis for comprising individual differences. The aggregating functions of party are more important at the legislative level than at the electoral level, for policies can only emerge as agreements to enact; the luxury of requiring a precise correspondence of policy with preference must be foregone. The executive does not face this difficulty of internal disagreement; hence whatever makes it harder for legislators to form permanent and effective coalitions is likely to increase the power of the executive. This is particularly true where the executive commands the attention of the media, thus exercising leverage through that very instrument that has gained in power from the rootlessness of political preferences.

On the other hand, to the extent that the executive influenced the legislature because he was head of the party that had a legislative majority, he will find the weakening of party ties an impediment to the exercise of this influence. Losing this source, he will need to rely upon his persuasive powers with all legislators, and may gain some powers of persuasion with the opposite party. Perhaps it will be the case that an executive whose party is different from the majority party in the legislature will now have more influence than he did before. Surely different working relationships will now be worked out, and the executive will find himself playing a somewhat different political game.

Future Politics

In political forecasts as in weather forecasts, persistence in forecasting is probably the best course. Things will not be all that different. Alienation will diminish as the Vietnam war declines, but the revolt against the constraints of organized society will continue. The headlines will be different, the expressions will take new forms, but the change of language will mask much sameness (the old Western sourdough's complaints about civilization have their current echo; the defection of the younger sons in an aristocracy has its analogs in the defection of the sons of the meritocrats). The protestors have hit on a set of weapons that are effective in a technologically tenuous society, but technology and adjustment will find ways of containing and turning the protests. No doubt the mild erosion of party, social class, and community cues for political guidance will create a period of fluidity; but structure has a way of coming back. The need for reliable working partnerships and coalitions and the need for predictable behavior will reimpose new sets of common expectations. The politics of the seventies will be different; but the differences will be within the framework of institutions and cultural norms that share much with the sixties and perhaps even more with the fifties and earlier periods of American history.

[1] Abraham H. Maslow, *Motivation and Personality* (New York: Harper, 1954) and *Toward a Psychology of Being* (Princeton, N.J.: Van Nostrand, 1968); Gordon Allport, *Becoming* (New Haven: Yale University Press, 1960).

[2] I am grateful to Mr. Libby of the political science department at the University of Washington for letting me see his insightful and imaginative paper suggesting the linkage between the findings of sense psychology and the explanations of alienation. In this paper, Libby deals principally with the theory of alienation developed by Kenneth Keniston in his *The Uncommitted: Alienated Youth in American Society* (New York: Dell, 1960) and the research reported in Phillip Solomon *et al.*, eds., *Sensory Deprivation* (Cambridge, Mass.: Harvard University Press, 1965).

[3] See my "The Political of Consensus in an Age of Affluence," *American Political Science Review*, Vol. LIX (1965), pp. 874-895.

Index

Computer analysts, 27
Computer letter, 13, 52, 145, 154, 158, 159, 167, 199
Computer output, 148
Computer simulations, 240-41
Computer telegram, 158
Computerized aggregate electoral data analysis, 200
Computerized data bank, 35
Congress, 15, 36, 84, 137, 138, 209, 226, 242, 245
Congressional elections, 261
Congressional Quarterly, 208
Congressional voting, 260
Connecticut, 22, 26, 132, 218
Conservatism, 58, 164, 229, 270
Constituency, 59
Continuous polls, 50
Convention of 1972, 31
Converse, Phillip, 250
Corrupt Practices Act, 138
Cost-effective analysis, 186, 195
Counter-culture, 277, 278, 288
County chairman, 24, 25
Cramer, Sen. William, 36, 41
Crime on the streets, 264
Culture of failure, 277
Currier, Frederick P., 143
Cybernetics, 284
Cynicism theory, 281, 282, 283, 285
Cyr, Picard and Associates, 115

D

Data analysis, 26, 128, 153, 157, 185, 201
Data processing, 150, 171
Declaration, 101, 102
Decline of the political party, 252, 256, 259, 297
Deep South, 85
Demand media, 245
Democratic, 86, 179, 215, 229, 247, 254, 255, 260, 261, 265
Democratic-Farmer-Labor party, 183-204
Democratic National Committees, 14, 20, 30, 32, 33, 34, 36, 144, 199
Democratic party, 14, 20, 33, 66, 254
Democratic Party Voter Registration Campaign, 144

Democratic Policy Council, 35
Democrats, 28, 32, 58, 82, 83, 84, 85, 87, 121, 131, 151, 160, 163, 188, 212, 213, 231, 259, 262, 264, 271, 288, 297
Demographic data, 13, 125, 163
DeSimone (R), Gov. Herbert F., 40
Detroit Free Press, 143
Detroit News, 154
DeVries, Dr. Walter, 39, 41, 136
Dewey, John, 222, 226-27
Direct mail, 35, 69, 78, 81, 154, 162, 165, 166, 167, 176, 202, 203
Direct personal appeal, 182
Dirksen, Sen. Everett M., 212
Dirty Politics, 210, 230, 231, 232, 233
Disclaimer, 45, 46
Disclosure, 227
Disorientation theory, 282, 285
Documentaries, 48, 70, 73
Domino theory, 294
Door-to-door campaigning, 192, 200
Douglas, Sen. Paul, 211
Doves, 132
Drugs, 85, 127, 175, 264
Duffey, Sen. Joseph, 40, 86

E

Ecology Issue, 88
Economic issue, 86, 87
Educational programs, 70
Eisenhower, Dwight D., 93, 94, 242, 246
Election of 1928, 255
Election of 1940, 249
Election of 1950, 210
Elections of 1958, 84, 160
Elections of 1960, 160, 161
Election of 1964, 222
Election of 1966, 186
Election of 1968, 34
Election of 1970, 25, 27, 36, 41, 55, 115, 131, 133, 138, 211, 262, 265
Elections of 1972, 156, 265
Election day, 180
Election polls, 117
Elections Research Center, 39
Electoral data analysis, 200
Electorate, 21

Independents, 17, 257
In-depth interviews, 127
Indiana, 23, 234
Inflation, 263
Information and communications system, 65
Information-gathering phase, 195
In-house radio service, 35
Instant information, 48, 150, 156
Intellectuals, 277
Interpersonal media, 68
Interpersonal orientations, 75
Interpublic Group Companies, 116
Iowa, 23
Irish Catholics, 231
Issue emphasis, 194
Issue politics, 75, 76, 126, 157, 170, 248, 252, 259, 261
Issue poll, 114
Issue research, 171, 200, 201
Issue training workshop, 193
Italians, 58

J

Jackson, Sen. Henry M., 85
Janowitz, Morris, 250
Javits, Sen. Jacob, 96, 98, 116
Jefferson, Thomas, 94, 95, 129
Jersey City, 255
Jewish districts, 174
Jews, 285, 287
Johnson, President Lyndon, 85, 121, 222, 246, 258, 264
Johnson, Nicholas, 94
Journalism, 184
Junk mail, 81

K

Kahn, Herman, 156
Keniston, Kenneth, 268, 280
Kennedy, Ethel, 98
Kennedy, President John F., 144, 246, 250-51, 268
Kennedy, Sen. Edward, 40
Kennedy, Sen. Robert, 96, 98
Key, Jr., V. O., 233
Kleppe, Sen. Thomas S., 41

L

Labor union members, 58
LaGuardia, Fiorello, 255
Landon, Alf, 245
Lane, Robert E., 239
Lang, Kurt, and Gladys Lang, 243
Law and order, 294
Laurent, Lawrence, 92
Lazarsfeld, Paul, 249
Lead time, 55
Legal aid in ghettoes, 292
Legislative behavior, 201
Legislators Campaign Handbook, 191
Lenin, 254
LeVander, Harold, 191-92
Liberal, 164, 229
Liberal candidate, 174
Liberalism-conservatism, 186
Libby, Ronald, 279-80
Licht, Gov. Frank, 40
Limitation on broadcast spending, 110
Lindsay, Mayor John, 58, 116, 171, 174, 178, 179, 180
Listening and viewing habits, 59
Literary Digest, 245
Literature, 192
Lithuanians, 58
Loaded words, 127
Local constituency level, 203
Local issues, 175
Local party leadership, 22, 24
Local party organization, 22, 202
Local precinct, 177
Local registration laws, 25
Long-range planning, 185
Lorenz, John d'Arc, 115
Lower-level campaigns, 202
Lower-middle-income, 81
Lucey, Gov. Patrick, 40

M

Machiasport, Maine, 88
Madison Avenue, 166, 241, 296
Magazine advertisements, 69, 70
Make-up person, 104
Mail (*See*: Direct Mail)
Mandel, Gov. Marvin, 38, 40
Market Opinion Research, 143, 151, 154

Republican governors, 63
Republican National Committee, 16, 20, 151
Research, 106, 118, 119, 120, 178, 185, 186, 201
Rockefeller, Gov. Nelson, 97, 218, 219, 220
Rockefeller, Gov. Winthrop, 220
Rogers, Will, 137
Romney, George, 39
Romney, Lenore, 39, 41
Roosevelt, President Franklin, 246, 250, 254, 255
Rootless politics, 273, 293, 297, 298
Roper, Elmo, 245
Rosenbloom, David, 248
Roudebush, Sen. Richard, 40, 212-13, 214, 234
Rules Commission of the Democratic National Committee, 14, 32, 33
Rural poor, 288
Russia, 254

S

Sacramento Bee, 209
Sampling techniques, 125
Sargent, Gov. Francis W., 40
Scammon, Richard, 39, 44, 74-75, 135, 267
Scheduling, 178
Schneider, John G., 94
Seconding speeches, 33
Selective mailing, 142
Selective registration, 25
Segmentation studies, 135-36
Selective presentation, 295
Senate, 26, 28, 39, 82, 83, 84, 138 (*See also*: Congress)
Sensory deprivation, 279
Seymour, Dan, 242
Shapp, Gov. Milton, 38, 215
Shopping center polls, 51
Sign preparation, 192
Simulmatics Corporation, 238
Simulation, 143, 247
Simulation models, 150, 153
Simulation research, 247
Sloganeering, 230, 294
Slum political machine, 252

Smith, Al, 231
Social issue, 75, 86
Sorauf, Frank, 182
Sorenson, Ted, 96
Sound-on film documentaries, 71, 73
South, 232
South Carolina, 88
Spanish Civil War, 269
Special ballots, 25
Split ticket, 87, 182, 258
Spot television campaign, 256
Spot television commercials, 93, 111, 216, 218, 294
Sportscast, 73
Spurt technique, 46
Squier, Robert D., 92, 99
State manuals, 24
Stennis, Sen. John, 233
Steffens, Lincoln, 253
Stevenson, Adlai, 94, 139, 242, 246
Stevenson, Sen. Adlai III, 40, 86
Stewart, John G., 20
Student blitz, 88
Students, 276, 292
Student sit-ins, 281, 285
Student unrest, 86
Straw vote polls, 50, 51, 129
Street protest, 285
Suburbs, 148, 256
Supreme Court, 13
Survey Research, 114, 117, 125, 127, 129, 171, 195, 196, 247
Survey Research Center, 249
Swing districts, 174
Swing voter, 151
Switch-split, 163, 164
Symington, Sen. Stuart, 28

T

Talk shows, 70, 74
Tammany machine, 255
Targeting, 51, 163
Target precincts, 142-43
Tariff, 267
Teeter, Robert, 157
Telenews technique, 49
Telephone, 154, 162
Telephone campaign messages, 69, 70
Telephone polls, 51, 142

U